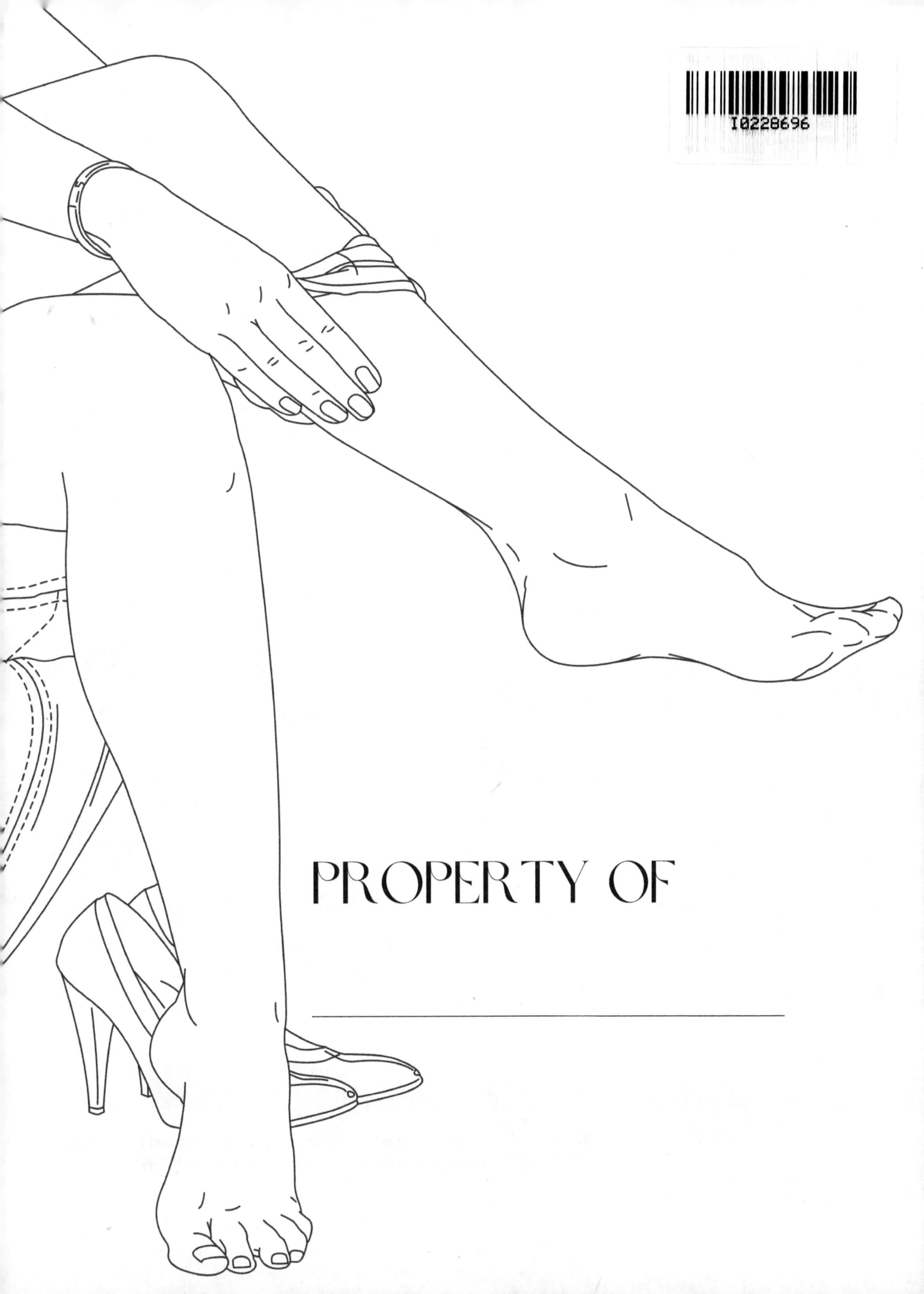

Copyright © 2022 Natasha Strange

All rights reserved. No part of this publication may be reproduced, stored in a retrieval system or transmitted in any form, by any means — electronic, mechanical, photocopying, recording or otherwise — without the prior written permission of the publisher.

KINK FOR THE CURIOUS
A BDSM ACTIVITY BOOK FOR BEGINNERS

by Princessa Natasha Strange

APPROACHABLE SHAME-FREE BDSM EDUCATION

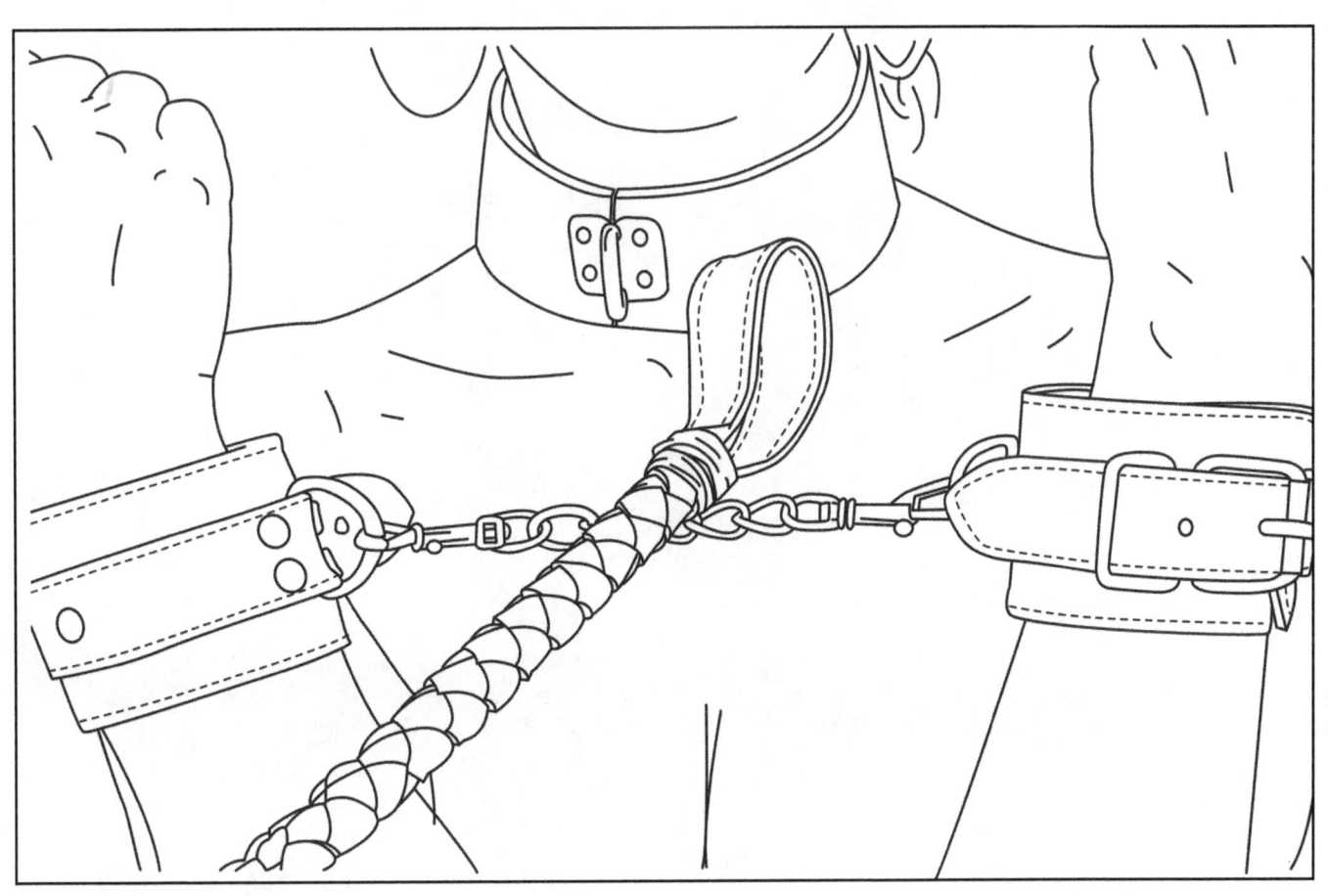

This book is dedicated to all the nervous newbies. The people who are terrified but feel the need to explore. The ones who aren't sure what they want but are willing to sample kink until they figure it out. The ones who shyly ask, then openly blossom. You are amazing.

Kink for the Curious is a fun-filled activity book intended to help you learn about yourself and your kinky interests. It's meant to be written and colored in, doodled on, and loved until its pages are worn. It's a place for you to document your journey so you can go back and read about your growth. It's your own special place to explore, reminiscent of the locking diaries you had as a child. Keep it private until you are ready to share.

In these pages, you will find bits of wisdom, journal pages, kinky color pages, and more. Although whimsical, each activity was designed to help you learn about and feel more comfortable in the world of kink.

Everything in this book works under two basic tenets.

First, **all activities are safe and consensual.**

Second, **there is no right, only what's right for you.** People ask me if they're doing spanking or training their submissive correctly. The answer is always the same. Is it safe and consensual? Is it working for you? Then yes, you are doing it right. While you should always learn proper technique and safety for the activities you are performing, the type of activities and the rules around them and your play, are yours to experiment with.

Kink and BDSM is play, for adults. And like play for children, as long as no one is going to get injured, it's being done correctly.

When we are young, we play. We explore our bodies and the world around us. When we grow up, we are expected to stop playing. Let's not. Let's continue to explore through kink and BDSM.

Play nice. Play hard. Play dirty.

NEVER STOP PLAYING.

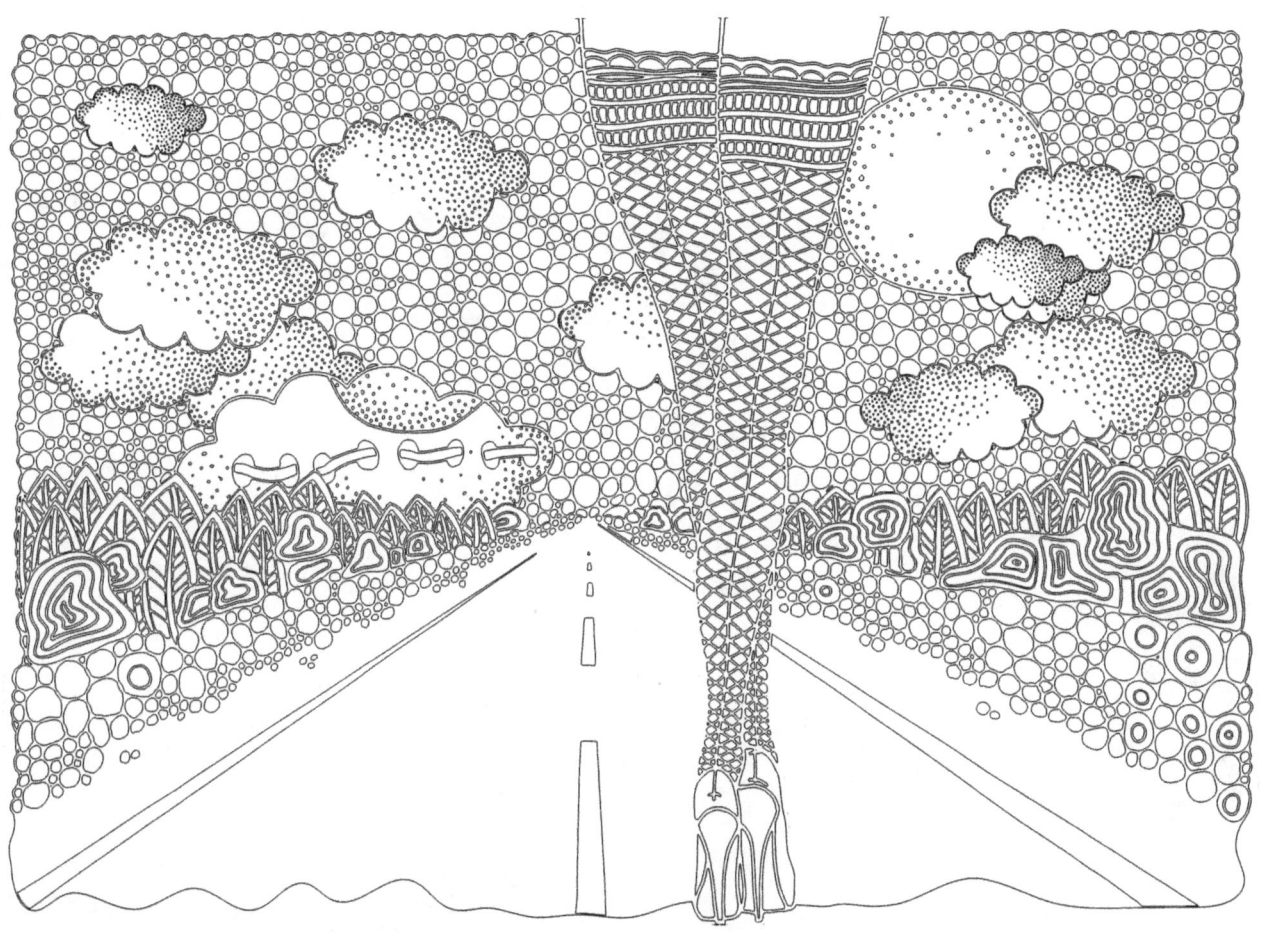

CONTENTS

KNOWLEDGE IS POWER ... 11

COMMUNICATION AND CONSENT ... 37

EXPLORING YOUR KINKY PERSONA ... 63

THE CYCLE OF PLAY ... 87

GAMES PEOPLE PLAY ... 107

ANATOMY OF A SCENE ... 147

CONTRACTS, OWNERSHIP, AND RULES ... 169

WORKSHEETS ... 187

PUZZLE KEYS ... 217

KNOWLEDGE IS POWER

Kink and BDSM is a huge arena. When you're just getting started, it can feel overwhelming. Take one step at a time. Once you get to know what you and your partner(s) are interested in, you can start to learn about those activities. You will never be expected to know everything. You are only required to know about you and your partner's kinks. As you explore and evolve, you can expand your knowledge and learn more. Sometimes activities that scare you become favorites once you know the intimate details.

After nearly three decades as a professional dominatrix, I still occasionally run across something new, and it's always a thrill to find unexplored fetishes and fantasies.

Start small and learn about the activities that interest you most. Everyone was, at one point, a nervous newbie. Even me. Keep an open mind and press forward. Hopefully by the time you have worked your

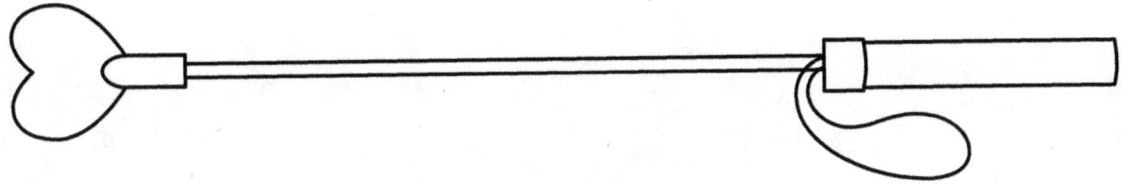

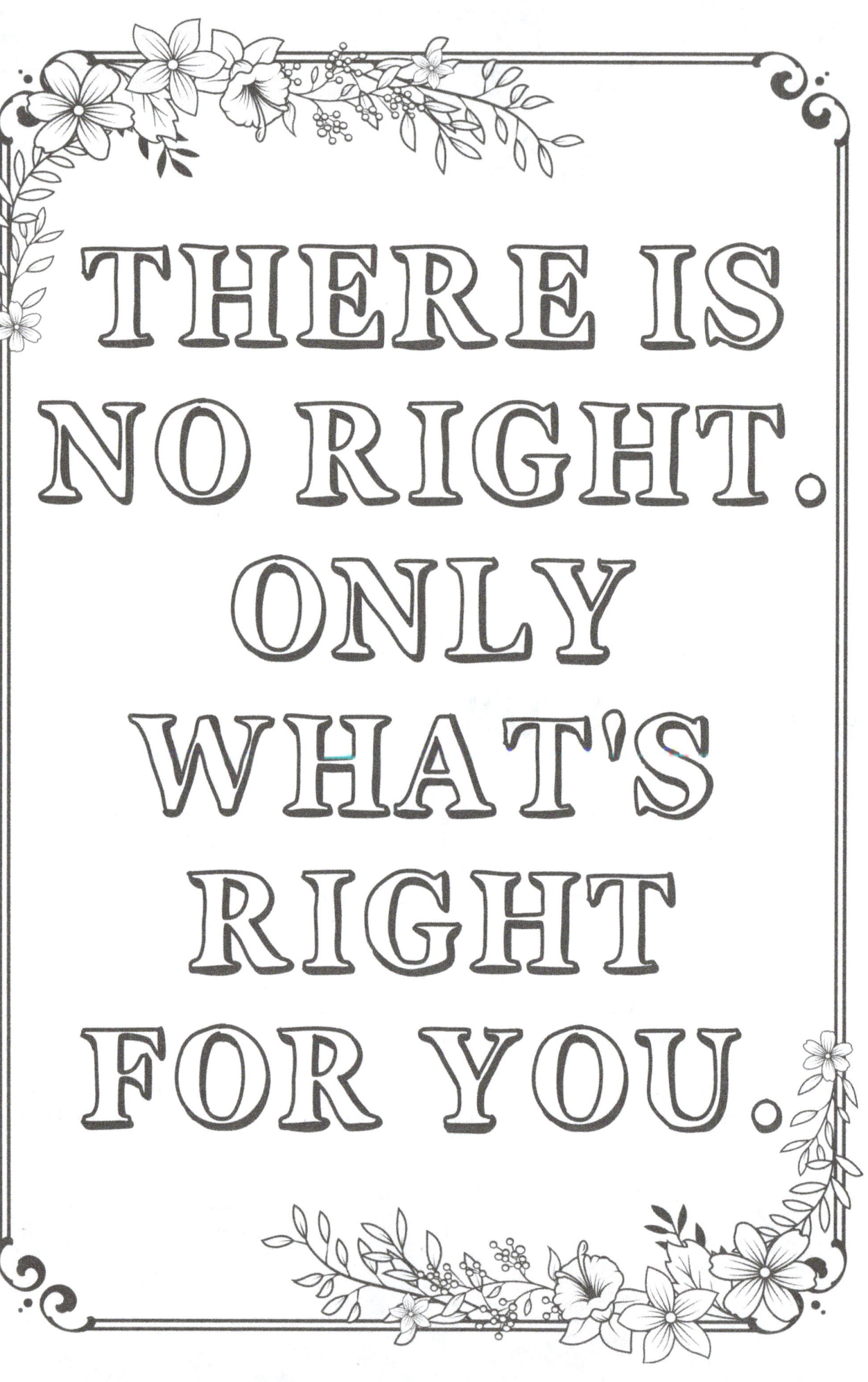

way through this book, you'll have a better understanding of where to begin and in which direction you want to go first.

WHAT IS BDSM & KINK?

BDSM is an all-encompassing abbreviation that stands for Bondage & Discipline / Domination & Submission / Sadism & Masochism, but includes other kinks like pony or puppy play, age play, and a wide range of fetishes that don't easily fall within any of those terms.

Bondage: Restraining people with rope, cuffs, or other tools.
Discipline: Adhering to rules and behavioral expectations, and paying the consequences when you fail.
Domination: The act of imposing your will on another.
Submission: The act of offering yourself, mentally and/or physically, to another.
Sadism: Joy and pleasure from inflicting pain.
Masochism: Joy and pleasure from receiving pain.

I like the word "kink" as an all-encompassing descriptor for people who are looking to explore and play in the bedroom. Kink can be something as simple as a flirty roleplay, or more involved, like a full night of bondage and impact play. Kink is about exploring your sexuality. Kink is full of pain, giggles, orgasms, bondage, worship, penetration, and a world of other physical and emotional sensations. Pain can be part of your play, but it doesn't have to be.

Much like children explore their bodies and the world around them through play, adults explore their bodies and the world around them in a more adult version of play. This is why, when I decided to write a textbook for my classes, I decided to model it after the activity books I loved as a child.

Just because this book is whimsical and cheery does not mean I believe all BDSM and kink is whimsical and cheery. Some is serious, dirty, nasty, sloppy, slutty, and dark. As long as it's safe and consensual, and all parties are aware of any risks involved, then you are doing it right.

There is no right. Only what's right for you. That doesn't mean there aren't proper ways to perform certain activities, like bondage or electrical play. It means there is no proper way to enjoy your kink and your play. There is no "right way" to enjoy being dominant. No "right way" to be submissive. No "right way" to be kinky.

WHY BRING KINK INTO YOUR LIFE?

Short answer? Because it's fun, and there are cool toys and amazing outfits!

Longer answer: Kink helps you get to know yourself. It requires self-examination to understand why

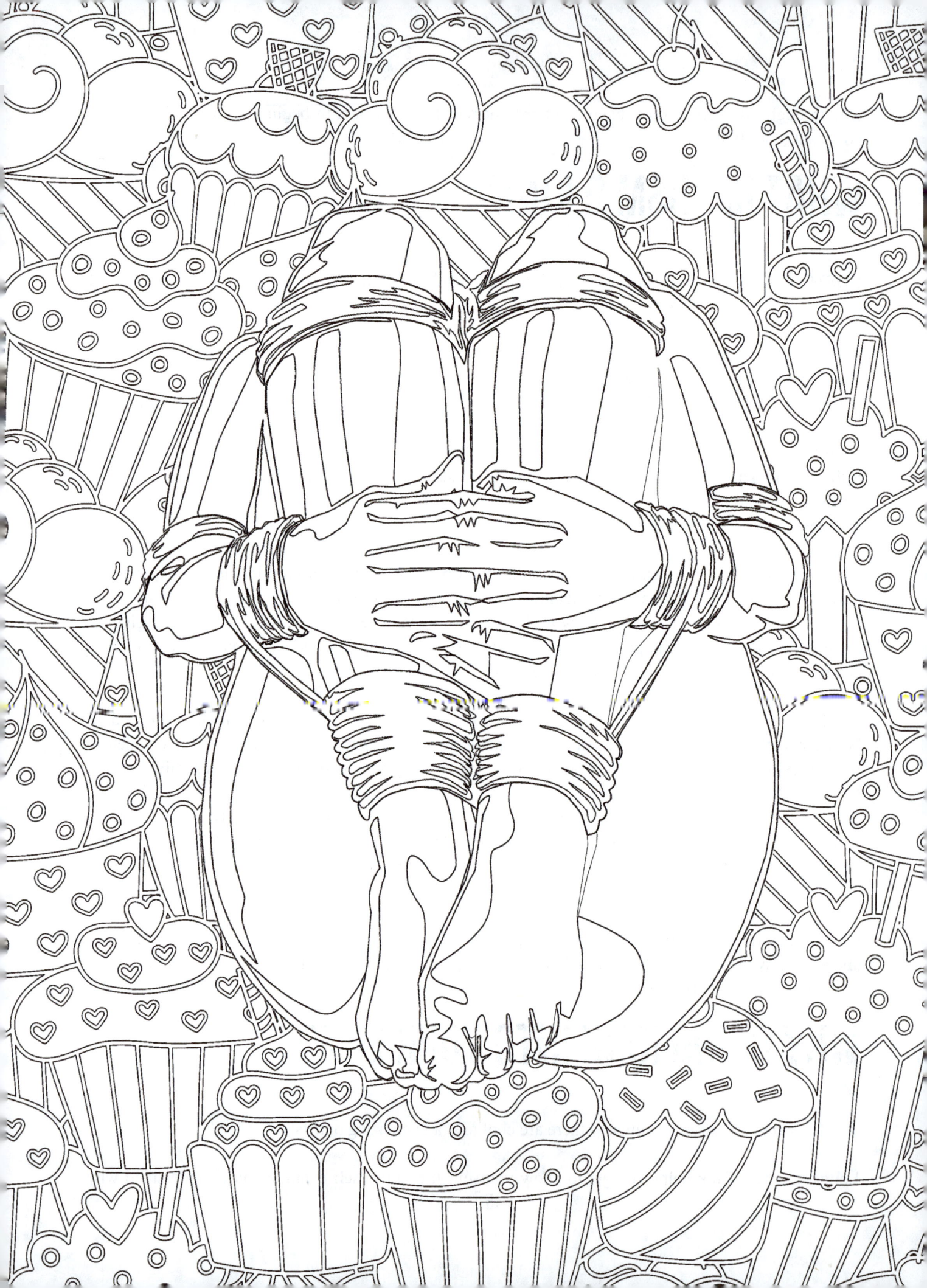

something turns you on or why it makes you uncomfortable. You need to learn about yourself to know what you want, what your limits are, then under what situations you are okay stretching those limits. Kink gives people a way to share a new sexy secret. It provides a chance to explore each other, mentally and physically. To create a secret language of sorts. While some people find vanilla sex satisfactory, others like to explore and push limits. They want stronger sensations. They need excitement. They crave exploration. Kink helps satisfy these needs.

Kink will also help you sharpen your communication skills. There is no simple "put Tab A in Slot B" in kink, so once you know yourself, your interests and your limits, you need to be able to communicate those ideas to your partner in a clear, concise way. As you practice discussing interests with your partner, you'll find it easier to discuss your day-to-day needs with those around you.

Getting to know yourself and sharpening your communication skills will increase your satisfaction in all aspects of your life. Not just your sex life.

WHY DOES THIS TURN ME ON?

The short answer is no one knows.

The long answer is varied. Some people can trace it back to something that happened when they were a child. Some developed their interests over time; others can't remember a time when they didn't think about their kink. Some people simply like the excitement of something new or the rush of trying something taboo. There is no right answer.

If you need to know why your particular kink turns you on, I would suggest talking to a kink-friendly therapist. Just because you have a kink or fetish does not mean there is something "wrong" with you. Having some sort of kink, fetish, or "non-standard" sexual interest is actually quite common.

TOPS, BOTTOMS, SWITCHES, AND TITLES

The top or dominant is the person who leads the play. A top is someone who like to do things to the other person. A dominant is someone who enjoys power over another. You can be either, or both at the same time. A top or dominant can choose whatever title they feel comfortable with. Some femmes like to be called Daddy for a little role-reversing gender-fuckery. Other femme tops simply like to be addressed as Ms., Mistress, Mx., Goddess, My Queen, or Chief Erotic Officer. Pick something that makes you feel good when others say it.

Hopefully they will be saying it a lot. With permission, of course!

A bottom is someone who likes things to be done to them. A submissive is a person who enjoys the act of being submissive in power exchange. Again, you can be either or both. Bottoms or submissives can choose, or have their top choose whatever title they are comfortable with. Slave, Slut, Princess Cum Bucket, and Cuntalicious Kitten have appealed to others.

Some people like to go back and forth between roles, which is referred to as "switching." If you're a switch, you can choose two names with two distinct personalities if you like, or simply stick with one name and title. Your scene name, and all the rules and etiquette associated with it, are yours to create and mold as you see fit.

Have fun choosing a name and title. It's going to be your secret bedroom superhero identity!

And finally, some people are fetishists who just like their particular item or roleplay and don't feel a connection to all the other trappings of kink. A good example are foot fetishists who simply like sex more when feet are involved.

Different people, situations, or activities may bring out your desire to be one or the other. Remember: There is no right, only whats right for you.

WHAT IS A PLAY PARTNER?

Play partners are the people we play with. Sometimes those are the people we are also in a traditional relationship with, and sometimes those are simply people in our lives who we enjoy our kinks with. Kinky friends with benefits. Play partners occasionally go on playdates, where the main purpose of the date is to indulge in kinky play. Play parties are social gatherings with the express purpose to dress up in fetishwear, and indulge in kinky activities.

Kinky people like to play.

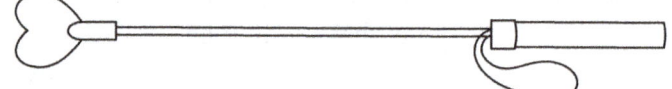

KINK AND SHAME

Some people feel ashamed because of their kinks. Sometimes, as you start experimenting, that shame will fade away. But some people find it gets more intense. Often, the best thing to do is to be open with your partner and talk about your shame. Shame thrives in secrecy, and bringing it into the open can banish it.

Shame can come from societal or family expectations. It can also come from the idea that "good girls don't" when in fact, most good girls do, to some extent. As you work through this book, hopefully you will find ways to eradicate your shame. If not, look for a kink-friendly therapist in your area. AASECT or American Association of Sexuality Educators, Couselors and Therapist is a good place to start that search. www.AASECT.org

SSC OR RACK OR FRIES? WHAT ?

There are differant ways to talk about your safety and consent standards. This is just the most basic breakdown of the top three you will hear. There are whole books written about consent in BDSM and long conversations to be had. If you have questions as to whether something is falls into your chosen guidelines, step back, reexamine. Get your questions answered and your concerns addressed before you start.

SSC stands for Safe, Sane, and Consensual. Old Skool and somewhat outdated but at the very least, serves as a guide.

SAFE: Will anyone die? Will anyone be arrested? Will people who have not had a chance to negotiate their involvement be affected? Will there be lasting marks or damage that hasn't been discussed and agreed to?

SANE: This can be a moving target. What you think is insane now will change. BUT, all parties involved should be capable of making decisions. A good rule of thumb is, could they legally sign a contract? Are they of age? Sober? Not under duress? Then it's sane.

CONSENSUAL: Have are all parties given consent to the proposed activities? Have they chosen a safe word? Have they voiced glee (even terrified glee) at the upcoming events? Are they able to give consent? You cannot give consent when you are drunk or under the influence. Not even Thursday night wine drunk.

RISK AWARE CONSENSUAL KINK: Risk-aware Consensual Kink or RACK, is similar yet different from Safe, Sane, and Consensual kink. Both rely on consent, but RACK acknowledges that there are risks with nearly every activity, from riding on a plane or playing catch with your kids, to exploring kink in the bedroom. Risk-aware Consensual Kink is the belief that all parties are fully informed of the risks.

I tend to stick with RACK and steer away from Safe, Sane, and Consensual. "Sane," in addition to being a moving target in our kink explorations, is an outdated word in general. We all have mental health struggles, big and small and very few of us are truly sane.

RACK also brings risk awareness into the conversation. Both the top and the bottom should always be aware of the risks of any kinky games you plan on playing.

FRIES, or Freely Given Reversible Informed Enthusiastic Specific is a updated version created by Planned Parenthood. From their website:

1. **Freely Given**: When consent is freely given, this indicates that there was no coercion involved and the person agreed to the particular activity at their own free will.

2. **Reversible**: Consent is always reversible, which means that a person may agree to an activity earlier in the day or week and then realize that they no longer want to proceed. If someone reverses their decision to partake in an activity, that does not mean to guilt them into proceeding. Their decision to stop should be respected!

3. **Informed**: Consent is always informed. This means knowing exactly what is happening before, during, and after the activity.

4. **Enthusiastic**: This is important when getting consent because only "yes" means "yes." If there is any uncertainty or hesitation, then stop.

5. **Specific**: This means to be firm in setting boundaries and making it clear about what you will or will not engage in.

As we evolve and learn, these will also be updated. You my identify with one of these more now, but deside another suits you in the future. Or you may find a forth not listed here that calls to you. That's the great thing about kink! It's all about evolving and finding what it right for you — and having the ability to change that when you need or want to.

POP QUIZ!

What style calls to you? Why?

_____
_____
_____
_____
_____
_____
_____
_____

MISCONCEPTIONS ABOUT KINK & BDSM

It's rarely practiced. **FALSE!** Studies suggest that somewhere between 30% and 40% of the U.S. and UK population has experimented with some aspect of BDSM or kink at some point in their life. Because of the shame and stigma around BDSM and kink, that reported number is probably low.

Participants are either dominant or submissive. **FALSE!** Many are switches, going back and forth between enjoying the dominant and the submissive role. Some people are dominant with certain people or during certain activities, but submissive at other times. Some people like to take turns switching and enjoy both sides.

BDSM is violent. **FALSE!** BDSM can be violent, but it doesn't have to be. Servitude, crossdressing, foot- worship, roleplay, tickling, adult baby play, slut training, medical play, and cuckolding are just a few of the many nonviolent ways to engage in kink and BDSM.

BDSM always involves sex. **FALSE!** That depends on your definition of sex. Neither penetration nor orgasm is always the end goal as it is with more traditional sex. BDSM incorporates a mental aspect that may not even require nudity or physical contact. Each relationship is different.

BDSM requires fancy tools and expensive equipment. **FALSE!** I got everything I needed to start at the local hardware store. So can you. The fancy toys are great, but open communication and consent, which are both free, are the only things that are mandatory.

You can tell if someone is dominant or submissive by how they act in everyday life. **FALSE!** Just because they're dominant in their everyday life doesn't mean they need to give up control in the bedroom. Sweet and shy in real life doesn't mean they're submissive. We're all special snowflakes.

Something is wrong with people who like BDSM. **FALSE!** Many studies show people who practice BDSM to be more well-adjusted than their vanilla counterparts. We spent way more time doing self-examination and understand our desires, needs, and limits.

Dominants are sadists, submissives are self-loathing. **Sometimes?** After proper negotiation. Yes. But not always. Being a good dominant requires a large amount of empathy. Giving up control to live your submissive fantasies can require a lot of personal strength.

BDSM is a new trend. **FALSE!** There are mentions of rituals of pain and ecstasy in cuneiform texts, the earliest form of writing. Read the origin of BDSM on Wikipedia. "Fifty Shades of Grey" has brought BDSM into the mainstream, but it's been bubbling along in the outskirts of polite society for quite some time.

The dominant partner has all of the control. **FALSE!** After negotiation — during which all partners are equal — the submissive gifts the dominant with their submission and an agreed upon safeword. If the submissive says their safeword during the play, the play ends, at least temporarily. Knowing that, who do you feel is in control?

FEELING LOST?

Finding your way in the world of kink and BDSM can be very confusing at times. You think you know where you're headed but find yourself going in a different direction. That's normal. It's all about the journey. As you get to know yourself and your partner(s), you will build trust and combine fantasies, resulting in a whole new adventure. An activity you thought you totally wouldn't like may become a favorite — but only with one person. Or only under certain circumstances. You may lose interest in a favorite activity as you learn about new ones. A story, dream, or idea will spark something, and you'll be off on a whole new adventure.

Go with it. Explore yourself. Explore your partner. Embrace your role as a Sexual Adventurer!

SAFEWORDS AND SAFETY SIGNALS

A safeword is a predetermined word that can be said any time play gets too intense, emotionally or physically in order to stop or pause the play. This can be time to give or receive any needed feedback, guidance, and reassurance. Safewords are traditionally used by submissives, but dominants can also have one, especially if they are starting out in a new or potentially uncomfortable activity.

There are exactly zero situations in which you should play without a safeword. Always set a safeword before you play, even if you don't think your play is going to get that intense. It's better to have it and not use it than to need it and not have it.

Safewords should be a word you wouldn't use in everyday conversation. This allows the submissive to beg for mercy and the dominant to know they are actually begging for more, unless they say the safeword. Same with bondage. Safewords are a way for the submissive or bottom to let the top know that there really is an issue and they aren't just trying to talk themselves out of their predicament.

Safewords can be leveled to help control the play. For example, by using "yellow" and "red." Yellow could be used to slow the play or indicate a problem. Red could be used to stop it.

Example: Yellow when receiving a spanking would mean "I'm reaching my limit," in which case the spanker would know to start bringing the spanking to a close or do something else for a bit, to allow their play partner to cool down before returning to spanking.

"Yellow on my right wrist" could mean that the bondage bottom's wrist was uncomfortable or too tight.

Red could be used when something in the play triggers one person in a way that they feel they need to stop and connect with their partner, or if an activity is more intense than they anticipated.

Or of course, you could just say GREEN! Let's go!

If the submissive has their mouth full or otherwise occupied, make sure they have a nonverbal safety signal. Snapping fingers, holding something they can drop, or opening and closing their fist rapidly all work well as nonverbal safety signals.

If the submissive says their safeword, the dominant needs to react immediately. It's just a time to learn about each other and deepen trust. The dominant learns more about what triggers their submissive. The submissive learns that they can trust their dominant to take care of them.

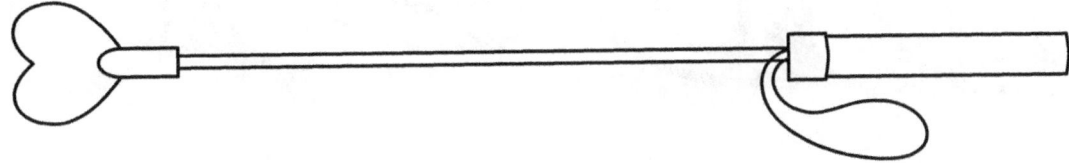

USING NUMBERS TO CHECK IN

Asking a submissive to rate where they are can help you gauge how they are feeling. Ask on a scale of 1–10 how close to their safeword they are. Even as they are guiding me, I try to keep the illusion that I am in control. If they reply 4, I tend to reply, "Good. You should have no problem reaching 9!" If they reply 8, I ask if they can reach 9. I enjoy a good mindfuck, so sometimes I'll ask if they can go to 11 while actually bringing the intensity down a bit.

A NOTE ABOUT ONLINE SAFETY

With so many fun places to meet people for kinky explorations online, let's take a minute to talk about online safety when signing up for these accounts and meeting people.

Fact Number One: If it's on the internet, there is a chance it will be found by the wrong person.

Fact Number Two: That being said, the internet is a massive space, and having someone you know stumble across your kinky online activity is unlikely if you live in a big city.

Fact Number Three: Most people who are meeting someone for kinky activities are normal people just like you looking for a deeper, kinkier connection.

Fact Number Four: Some people are just assholes and will be even more of an a-hole on the internet where they can be an anonymous a-hole.

Fact Number Five: Sometimes these a-holes leave the comfort and safety of their computer and venture into the wild to make your life a living hell.

Fact Number Six: The only way to remain completely safe is to leave the world completely unexplored.

You, and only you, know what your balance is between exploring and feeling safe. That being said, there are ways to keep yourself safer. Many of these may seem obvious, but it's always good to have a primer before heading on your kinky way.

- Create and use an online kink persona with a different name and unrecognizable avatar.
- Always make sure someone knows where you're going and who you're meeting.
- Have a check-in time—e.g., I'm meeting them at noon. Expect a call from me by 12:15.
- Have a secret safeword that you can use with your friend—e.g., if you say "pickles" during your check-in call, you don't feel safe or comfortable.
- Meet in a public place.
- Be responsible for your own transportation.
- Limit alcohol intake.
- Don't leave your food or drinks unattended.
- And always, trust your gut.

SAFER SEX

Once you know what type of play you are interested in, it is your responsibility, top or bottom, to learn how to keep yourself and your partner physically safe and free from infection. If you are part of a fluid-bonded couple—a couple that only exchanges bodily fluids with each other—then some of these are not as pressing, but you still need to be aware of when and where you might run into bad bacteria and viruses.

If there is a possibility of fluid being transferred from one person to the other via toy, mouth, hand, etc., there is a possibility of infection. There are simple precautions to take to protect yourself and your partners.

Are you sharing your insertable toys with others? Use a condom on them. Can't use a condom on it? Find out how to sterilize it. Can't sterilize it? Find out where to buy it in bulk.

Did you draw blood with your whip, cane, or other impact toy? Know how to clean that type of material.

Leather can be sprayed down with antibacterial cleanser or 10% bleach mix, but it's porous and can't be 100% sterilized.

Metal, glass, and silicone can be boiled.

Wood depends on the finish. If it's sealed with a finish, you can clean it the same way you would clean leather. If it's not sealed, it may be impossible to clean, and you should only use it with that person in the future.

If you're engaging in electrical play, you need to know how to clean each piece depending on where it was used. For strap-on or pegging play, you need to know how to clean your particular harness and dildo. If you're doing rope play, you need to know how to clean your ropes, depending on how they were used.

Every game requires different toys.

Every toy requires different cleaning processes.

There are a million combinations. It is your responsibility, whether you play as a top, or a bottom, to know how to clean the toys you play with.

The items I will recommend you always have on hand are:

- Non-latex or nitrile gloves (available in the medical supplies section of the drug store)
- Dental dams
- Condoms
- Spray bottle of isopropyl 70% alcohol for sterilizing most serfaces and toys
- Lube! Try several and find one you enjoy.
- Safety scissors for rope or other binding games—packing wrap, scarves, or nylons
- Puppy pads (to cover furniture)
- Baby wipes and paper towels
- Soap and water

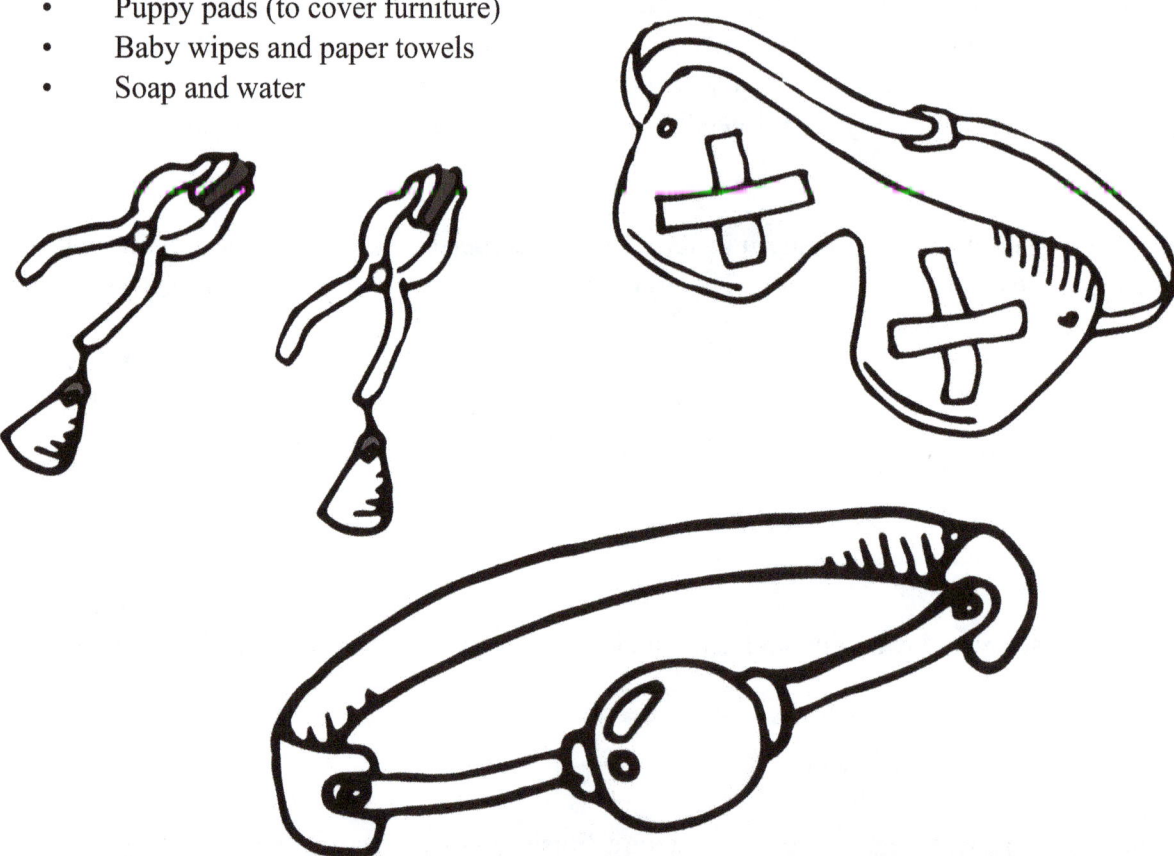

SAFEWORDS

The solution is in the back of the book

Arrange the safewords in the puzzle. If a letter falls in a box with a number, write it above the corresponding number below to reveal a secret message.

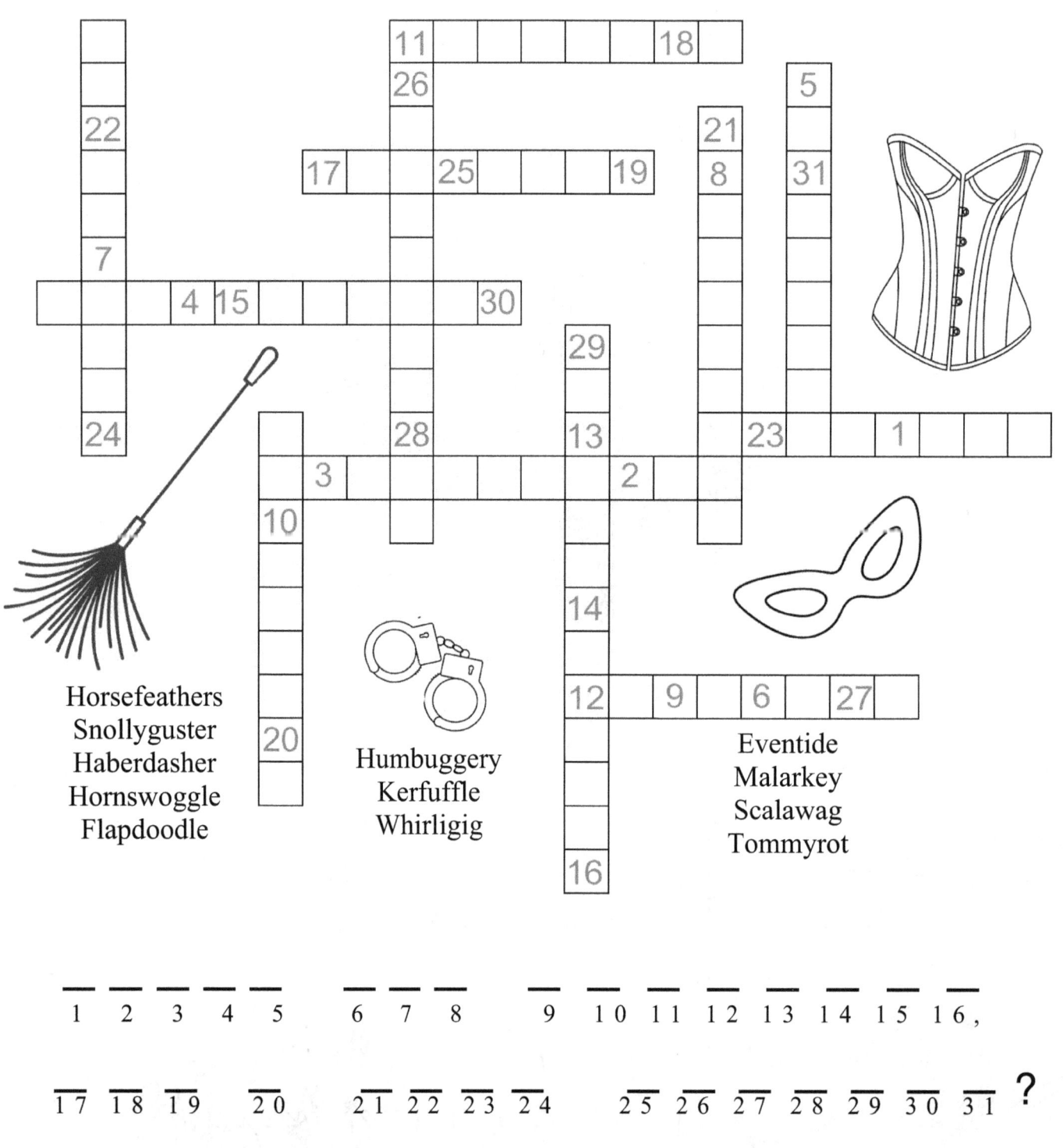

Horsefeathers
Snollyguster
Haberdasher
Hornswoggle
Flapdoodle

Humbuggery
Kerfuffle
Whirligig

Eventide
Malarkey
Scalawag
Tommyrot

__ __ __ __ __   __ __ __   __ __ __ __ __ __ __ __,
 1 2 3 4 5   6 7 8   9 10 11 12 13 14 15 16

__ __ __   __   __ __ __ __   __ __ __ __ __ __ __ ?
17 18 19 20   21 22 23 24   25 26 27 28 29 30 31

[28]

PHYSICAL SAFETY

When pain is involved in BDSM, the goal is to hurt but not damage. It doesn't matter if you're the top or the bottom, you are responsible for your own physical safety. You are also responsible for the safety of your play partner.

Yes. It sounds complicated, but it's not once you understand the basics.

If your top forgets that you have a shoulder injury and starts to bind you in a position that you know will irritate your shoulder, it's your responsibility to say your safeword and politely remind them. Even the best top may, at some point, forget or overlook something.

When you're in subspace, completely handing yourself over, body and soul, to your top, it can be difficult to correct them, but as your mentor, I give you permission. Permission to put your safety first, and permission to your top to punish you if you do not put your safety first. Your top should always be supportive of you putting your safety first.

As a top, it is your responsibility to respect your bottom's physical limitations. Submissives are often caught up in the need to please, and will suddenly find themselves agreeing to anal sex, beating, or other activities they know they'll regret once the scene is over. It is the top's responsibility to make sure the submissive doesn't violate their limits or take more than they can while under the heady influence of subspace.

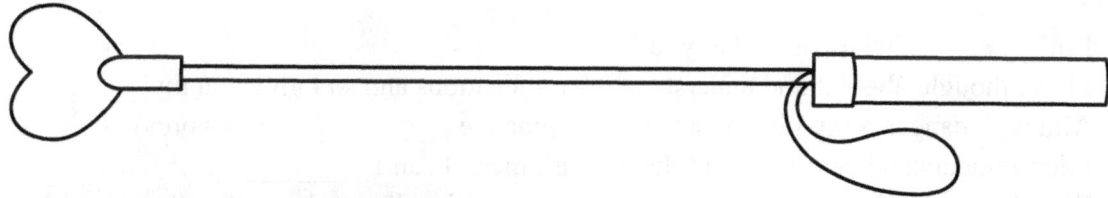

EMOTIONAL SAFETY

Treat emotional safety exactly like physical safety. If you find a particular type of play triggering and your top forgets and starts down that path, your safety comes first. Speak up and say your safeword. Do not think that it will pass or that you can take it "just this once." A good top will respect your limits and appreciate a reminder if they have a lapse in memory.

As a top, it is your responsibility to provide a safe space for your plaything to explore. Sometimes those activities are going to be taboo. If you are uncomfortable, it's your responsibility to protect yourself while also respecting their desires and not making them feel like there is something wrong with them. Likewise, if your plaything seems more eager once play is well underway to do something they were previously against, you need to understand if they are trying to please you.

RISK AWARE, CONSENSUAL KINK

THE SOLUTION IS IN THE BACK OF THE BOOK

Across:
3. It's okay to move them. But you should always know where they are.
5. Consent is _____.
8. Rape and blood play are types of _____. (two words)
9. Talking to you about my kinks makes me feel very _____.
11. Important in the real world, essential in the dungeon.
13. Like a condom for your mouth.
15. After I submit to you, I sometimes have this.
17. It sounds enticing; maybe when the time is right. (two words)
19. I've asked politely, I've waited, and now you have given me your _____ _____. (two words)
23. I want to treat you like the whore you are, but first I need to earn your _____.
26. Tops need it. Bottoms need it. Even that guy I just peed on needs it. (two words)
28. _____ flourishes in the dark.
29. For those who like to get their hands dirty.
30. Little reminders can have big implications.
31. I understand I may get injured or hurt. But I still want to proceed. (four words)
33. Waiting for this is difficult for you, but sexy for me.

Down:
1. I'm _____ with you, not at you.
2. I have thought about it and understand the implications and so I give you my _____.
4. Although danger is my middle name, I still practice _____. (two words)
6. I don't understand your kink, but that doesn't mean I can't _____.
7. We all need one in case things get too intense, emotionally or physically. (two words)
10. Even when pushing limits and boundaries, it's possible to practice _____. (two words)
12. Creating this can be difficult, but it helps communication flow freely.
14. Doing this fuels the sexiest kinky relationships.
16. While we could all use this, it's especially important for squeaky wheels and assholes.
17. Playing safe means having these on hand at all times. (3 words)
18. To explore my dirtiest fantasies with you, I need to feel _____.
20. Nope. I've no interest in that. Not now. Not ever. (two words)
21. One of the best skills to have in the dungeon.
22. Even though I am hurting you, you still have my respect and my _____.
24. Safe, Sane, and _____.
25. I wanted this, but you wanted that. We talked about it and have happily settled in the middle.
27. I freaked out and said my safeword. I just need a minute to catch my breath. Thank you for_____.
32. That big O in your wallet.

COMMUNICATION AND CONSENT

A SEXY TRUTH BOMB

We grow up with romantic movies and books telling us that if our partner REALLY loves us, they'll read our minds and know our bodies better than we do. Porn confirms those ideas.

I'm here to confirm what you have probably already figured out: That is complete bullshit.

Your partner, no matter how much they love you, and no matter how attracted to you they are, only knows as much about your body and your desires as you can communicate to them. If you don't spend time, possibly alone with porn, erotica, and/or sex toys, getting to know your body, you won't know your desires or your body and will have no way to communicate your needs. So my first assignment is to grab some kinky porn, books, or videos, some sex toys you are curious about, and go play with them!

Your body is a fancy fucking race car. Don't expect a stranger to hop in and know how to drive it properly.

Side note? Fancy fucking race cars occasionally need lube. Yup. Even yours. That doesn't mean you're not ready to race, er, fuck. It just means your hormones may be doing something else that day.

FOUR COMMUNICATION BASICS

Have patience. Be honest. Put the work in. Laugh with, not at.

Kinky communication can be difficult. Opening up about interests that you have kept secret for so long and that you can't quite put into words can take time. Don't expect to get everything perfect the first time.

Patience. Your partner may not be able to put their desires into words. They may need to experience activities before they can say what it is that they like or don't like about them. Even then, it can take time to process the associated emotions. As you gain experience, vocabulary, and self confidence in your new games, these communications will get easier and more direct.

Honesty. Be honest about your interest and experience level. If you say you have more experience than you do, your partner will expect more from you than you will be capable of giving. If you downplay your experience, because you are worried about coming off as too kinky or too experienced, your partner may not push you as far as you need to be pushed, and no one wants that!

You also need to be honest about your interests. If you want to be tied up and live out a kidnapping fantasy, the only way you your partner will know is if you tell them. They won't pick up on hints. You have to use your words. You might not want to lead with your most extreme fantasies, but if you do not voice them, you will not live them. Conversely, if something your partner is interested in doesn't turn you on, you need to be open and honest about that as well.

- Perhaps there is one aspect of it you do like.
- Perhaps it ends up being something they do on their own.
- Perhaps it's something they do with someone else. (Research ethical non-monogamy if you think that's a possibility for you.)
- Perhaps it's something you do on special occasions.
- Perhaps it's something you realize that you do like once you experiment a bit.

You can participate in an activity you don't fully enjoy to please your partner, but you need to be honest with yourself and your partner when doing so and expect the same level of compromise from them.

If you really don't enjoy an activity, practice self-care and don't participate, not even to make your partner happy.

Put the work in. Both parties need to be open and honest about their interest. Both parties need to do a lot of self-examination. Both parties need to work to keep communication open and shame-free. One person can't do all the work.

Laugh with. Not at. Laughing with your partner is a bonding experience. Laughing *at* your partner is a violation of trust. Unless that's their fetish and you've negotiated properly! Giggling at a fetish you don't understand means that if it IS something your partner is interested in, they aren't going to talk to you about it.

BOUNDARIES

Boundaries can move depending on where you are emotionally with the relationship. You should always be aware of your boundaries, communicate them, and stick to them. There are two basic types of boundaries: hard limits and soft limits.

HARD LIMITS

Hard limits are limits that are nonnegotiable. Examples include:

- Physical limitations. A shoulder issue prevents binding their arms overhead.
- Mental limitations. I was molested as a child and will not be involved in any kind of age play.
- Relationship limitations. I can play with you—spanking, bondage, etc—but have promised my partner there would be no penis-in-vagina type sex.
- Health limitations. I have asthma and breath play isn't safe.
- Just Fucking Because. I just don't find that sexy.

SOFT LIMITS

Soft limits are fluid. They can change based on interest level, relationship status, or how safe someone feels in the relationship. Examples include:

- I'm curious about that type of play, but I'm not ready.
- I only do that type of play with people I know really well.
- I don't want marks. I like the idea of marks, but I'm scared of that much pain. Perhaps for a special occasion.
- I like the idea of public play, but until I know you better, I'm not ready for it.
- I have rape fantasies, but that type of play is too intense for me at this point in my life.

Soft limits are to be explored, consensually. Hard limits are to be respected.

Something can be a soft limit one day and a hard limit the next. You are free to change and move your boundaries as often as you need to, even in the middle of play. If you thought an activity was going to be fine but once you begin you realize you are uncomfortable, you can back out. **Consent can be revoked by any partner at any time for any reason.**

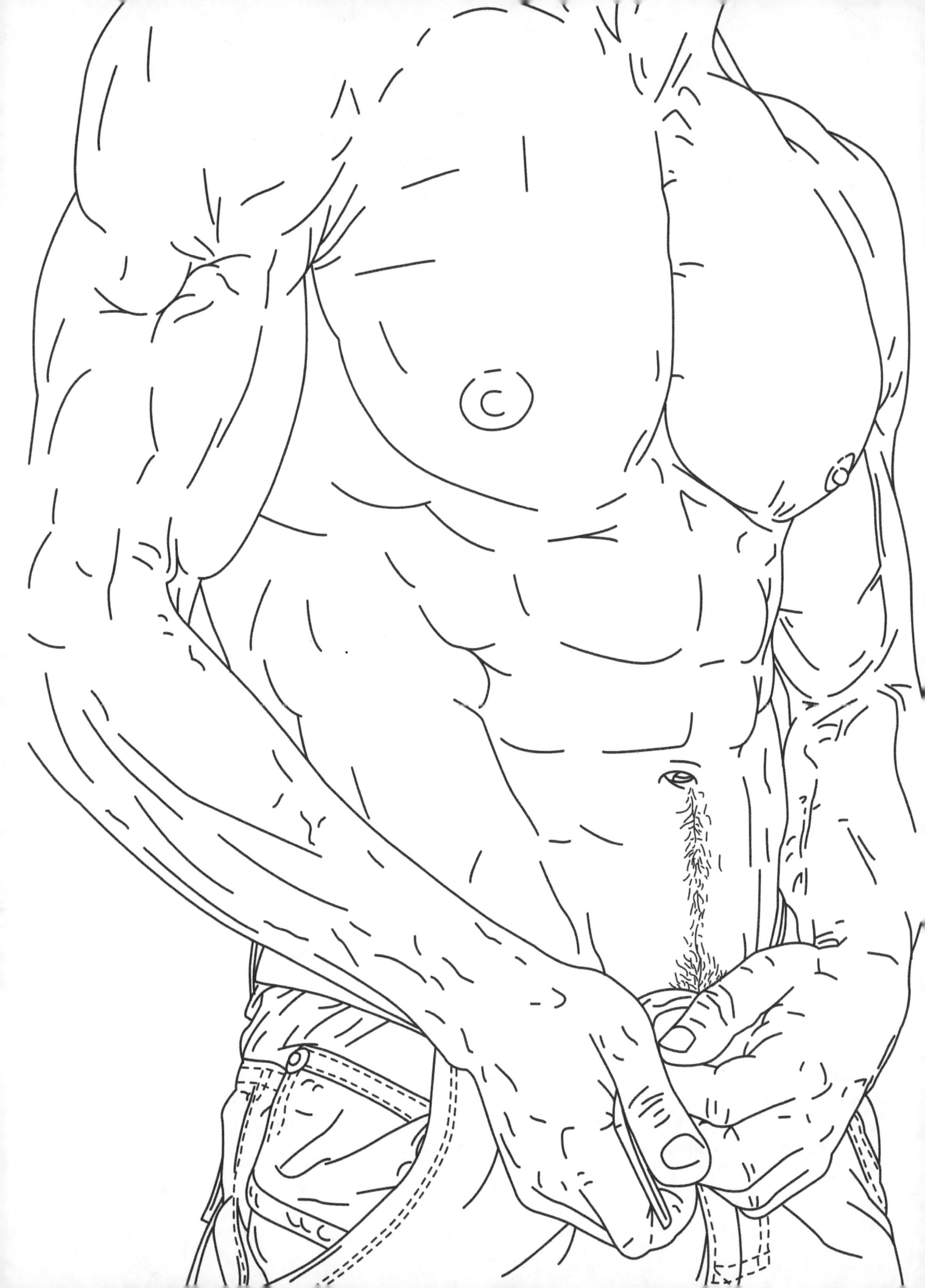

COMMUNICATION. FLOWER OR FLOUR?

One of the tricky things in BDSM and kink is that the words you say inspire different meanings to different people. This is why communication is so important. You can't just ask to be tied up. You're thinking hands tied overhead while your partner teases you with their tongue. Your partner is thinking of you hogtied with a plug shoved in your ass. While both might be of interest, clarification is always best!

When talking to your partner, always ask for clarification. If they say they like to do role-reversal, ask them what it means to them. You may be thinking boss/secretary roleplay, and they may be thinking taking turns spanking each other.

They may express an interest in foot worship, and you may picture them licking the dirty soles of your feet while you laugh at them, while they are fantasizing about massaging your feet while you masturbate.

Or the subject of bondage comes up and you're thinking shibari rope bondage and being suspended, helpless, while they are thinking strapped to the bed, spread eagle.

COMMUNICATION HOMEWORK

This requires a partner, or three. The goal is to understand the different ideas each word can inspire. Each person receives a sheet of paper and a writing utensil. Without discussion, or looking at your partner's work, each of you should write down four or five words you associate with each word below. Try to include at least one emotion, one physical sensation, and one location on your body or body position.

Spanking

Bondage

Dildo

Gag

Fetish

Flogging

Dominant

Submissive

Wet

Penatration

Dungeon

CONSENT AND TRUST BUILDING

When someone gives consent to do something and that consent is respected, hard limits aren't pushed, and proper aftercare is given, trust is built. Sometimes it takes a while to build that trust, but when that trust is built, fed, and nourished with respect, boundaries will shift, and deeper fantasies can be explored.

If you are really wanting to explore something intense but your partner is hesitant, give them time. Let them lead. Respect them when they say they aren't ready. Perhaps they will never be ready, and you need to be prepared to deal with that. But, should you earn their respect and build that trust, the play you can have will be worth the wait.

Building that trust takes time, effort, and communication. There is no shortcut, and violating someone's trust will set you back indefinitely.

This is true in the outside world, but even more so in the kink world.

TYPES OF CONSENT

Consent is a tricky thing. It's not as simple as asking. In kink and BDSM we need to be aware of the different types of consent that are possible.

You consented to going to Great Aunt Mildred's for Thanksgiving even though her turkey is dry—and the conversation? Even more so.

You consented to blowing that guy on your first date. But he was begging you to, and besides, by the end of the night you were so drunk it was sort of fun.

You will dog-sit the neighbor's aging dog even though you know it will mean scrubbing your floors despite getting up to let it out four times a night.

Consent is complicated. Don't give consent because you think it will make the other person happy. Don't give consent because you are afraid of hurting someone's feelings. Don't give consent to be nice. Drunken consent is not consent, no matter how enthusiastic.

As a bottom, only give consent because you want to consent.

As a top, you should always pay attention to the reason your bottom is consenting. Do they just want to please you? Are they trying to make you happy? Are they afraid to say no? Are they intoxicated?

As a top, it is your responsibility to understand your submissive's consent.

KINKY POP QUIZ

The solution is in the back of the book

Let's play with what we've learned so far! Find all the words hidden across, down, diagonally, and occasionally backwards.

```
L S I M N O I S S I M B U S G E
I E L O S O S P L E A S U R E N
E A E A P I A N C L A L B S B I
E R L R N I D N O F C P I O F L
P S D L N G E A E I T T P O L P
L A O D A I I R S N T T P U Y I
A F O T T U S S E C U A B G Y C
Y E D A C E G M Y M O R S T W S
P W P M X E E H A T I N S N K I
A O A E O T P S T C E E D S E D
R R L I I B O S A E N F M O V S
T D F C O C L T E O R D A H M J
N S X T H T I E H R P O T S X S
E E T I T O N N S B O N D A G E
R O S T N D O M I N A T I O N Q
M M A S T I M I L T F O S L Z E
```

BONDAGE	LAUGHTER	SADISM
BOTTOM	LUBRICATION	SAFER SEX
CONDOMS	MASOCHISM	SAFETY SIGNALS
DISCIPLINE	PAIN	SAFEWORDS
DOMINATION	PATIENCE	SENSATIONS
EXCITEMENT	PLAY PARTNER	SOFT LIMITS
FLAPDOODLE	PLEASURE	SUBMISSION
HONESTY	RESPECT	TOP

OWNING YOUR PLEASURE

The only way kinky communication can work properly is if both people acknowledge and talk about their pleasure openly. All parties involved must be able to talk about what they truly enjoy. It's fine to hold back until you're ready. But it won't happen until you are honest about your interests and needs. It takes two (or more!) people to communicate their interests, fantasies, and limits in order to make kinky play come to life.

HOW TO INTRODUCE YOUR PARTNER TO YOUR KINK

During sex with dirty talk. Passion lowers your inhibitions. Start the conversation with dirty talk in the heat of passion and see where it goes. Leave the action until later, when you can talk about what might actually be explored and what should remain dirty talk.

With porn, erotica, or pop culture references. Although not a huge fan of "Fifty Shades of Grey," I love the conversation that it's inspired. Referring to something in a movie or book and telling your partner that you are curious about it is sometimes easier than starting cold with "I have this reoccurring kinky fantasy."

Find a class about a fetish or idea you want to explore and ask your partner if they have any intereest in taking it with you. Sometimes learning together leads to bonding and more exploration, and taking a class with others who are also interested in those ideas can be a good way to destigmatize kinky play.

Over dinner with a glass of wine. Alcohol will lower the inhibitions and allow your conversation to get a little more open, in both directions. Be careful not to overindulge or you may end up having to have that conversation a second time, with a headache. And always remember, drunken consent is not consent.

ACTIVE LISTENING

We're used to interjecting with "Me too!" and an anecdote because most people are much better at talking than at listening. Active listening is an important tool in kink communication.

When you ask your partner a question, take a pause, wait 20 seconds—which will seem like an uncomfortably long time if you aren't used to it—and give them mental space to talk. Often, especially in sensitive areas like kink, where people are used to holding back, giving them those extra seconds of awkward silence will give them time to put words to the thoughts and feelings racing through their mind.

Respond to their answers with questions if you need more information. "How does that make you feel?" and "What does that mean to you?" are good open-ended responses that can help continue the conversation.

Listening like that—truly listening—is a very powerful tool which helps create a space of trust. As a professional dominatrix, I enjoy giving

people those uncomfortable silences, partly because I like making submissives squirm in discomfort, but also because it lets them know that I'm giving them space to share their thoughts and feelings, and putting a priority on listening to them. More importantly, it lets them know that I expect more. Occasionally, at the end of the 20 seconds, I will follow up with "Is that all?" and give them another 20 or so seconds to confess darker, more closely held secrets.

Because there are always more secrets.

IF YOUR PARTNER WON'T OPEN UP

Be patient. Be open. Be honest.

Talk about your own curiosities. Read erotica together. Watch porn together. Take a class at the local sex toy or adult book store together. If you don't have a local space that offers classes, look online for a virtual class that interests you both.

Give them time and space.

Unfortunately, there isn't anything you can do to get a partner to open up about their own fantasies aside from providing them a safe, non-judgmental place to talk. They need to do the work and learn how to talk to you.

A VERY IMPORTANT MESSAGE

The solution is in the back of the book

BDSM and Kink-land is vast, but with this information as your compass, you will never be lost.

At the top there is a key that lists all the letters from A thru Z with a box below. Each of the letters has a corresponding number. The bottom part contains a secret phrase. Each of the blanks has a number underneath it. Fill in the letters that correspond to the numbers below the blanks to solve the phrase. This is a difficult puzzle so there is a hint at the back of this chapter.

A	B	C	D	E	F	G	H	I	J	K	L	M	N	O	P	Q	R	S	T	U	V	W	X	Y	Z

__ __   __ __ __ __ __   __ __   __ __   __ __   __ __ __ __ ,
6 3   24 9 4 18   6 3   5 22   5 3   3 6 12 19

__ __ __ __   __ __ __   __ __ __ __ __ __ __ __ __ ,   __ __ __ __ __
3 6 4 19   6 4 16   25 9 4 3 19 4 3 21 6 24   22 13 19 7 19

__ __   __ __   __ __ __ __ __ ;   __ __ __ __ __   __ __   __ __ __ __
5 3   4 9   7 5 18 13 22   22 13 19 7 19   5 3   9 4 24 8

__ __ __ __   __ __   __ __ __ __ __   __ __ __   __ __ __ .   __ __ __
10 13 6 22   5 3   7 5 18 13 22   12 9 7   8 9 21   6 4 16

__ __ __ __   __ __   __ __ __ __ __   __ __ __   __ __ __   __ __ __ __
10 13 6 22   5 3   7 5 18 13 22   12 9 7   8 9 21   10 5 24 24

__ __ __ __ __   __ __ __ __   __ __ __ __   __ __ __   __ __
25 13 6 4 18 19   10 5 22 13   22 5 20 19   6 4 16   6 3

__ __ __   __ __ __ __   __ __ __ __ __ __ __ __   __ __ __
8 9 21   18 6 5 4   1 4 9 10 24 19 16 18 19   6 4 16

__ __ __ __ __ __ __ __ __ .
19 2 11 19 7 5 19 4 25 19

[50]

IF YOUR PARTNER DOESN'T UNDERSTAND YOUR KINK

Not everyone is going to understand your needs and curiosities, and that's okay. What is not okay is having someone, even your partner, shame you for them. It's all right for them to say "I don't think I'm into that." It's not all right to say "Ew! Gross! You're weird!"

Your interests are not gross.

You are not weird.

Having some sort of power exchange-based sexual curiosity or fetish is extremely common.

WHAT DOES THAT MAKE YOU THINK OF?

Sometimes when two people are talking about the same thing, they can be picturing it completely differently from each other. When talking about kink with your partner, the question "What does that make you think of?" is a good way to make sure you aren't thinking light, fluffy bondage while they're thinking dark and ominous. Even if you aren't on the same page, it can give you a good starting point.

LEARNING TO COMMUNICATE

There is no quick and easy way to learn to communicate. It takes time and practice. Learn from misunderstandings and be gentle with yourself and your partner(s). Look at intent. Did they mean to hurt your feelings? Or was there a miscommunication? We all misunderstand and misspeak once in a while. Part of the process is moving forward and listening to what your partner is saying, clarifying any questions, and not making assumptions. Sometimes we need to hear difficult things or say difficult things, but not saying them or refusing to listen to them doesn't change them.

PHYSICAL VS EMOTIONAL FEELINGS

From the outside it might feel as if BDSM and kink are all about physical feelings, but in reality, emotional feelings are the most important. Always find out how you and your partner want to feel emotionally before working on physical sensations.

Example: Spanking

Spanking seems like a simple physical act, but without understanding the emotions the spanking is meant to evoke, you can't give a proper spanking.

- Are you a naughty schoolgirl being punished?
- A slave being used?
- A lover being explored?

Do you like to spank as part of an escapist roleplay? Or as a way to feel powerful as you pin down a struggling submissive?

Once you have the feelings and intent down, you can move on to physical feelings. Stinging slaps with a hand? Or thudding wallops with a paddle? Long, slow warmup? Or a sudden, intense onslaught?

Example: Bondage

Does the bottom wish to feel helpless? Terrified? Excited? Silly? Do they want to be left to linger in bondage? Or it is the act of having their freedom of movement slowly taken from them that intrigues them? Is it a part of a superhero roleplay?

- Were they kidnapped and tossed into the back of a car?
- Did they enter into the bondage willingly? Or were they forced?
- Were they seduced into bondage?
- Do they want to feel like you bound them to punish them?
- Is bondage a reward?

Does the top relish the detail and skill required to decorate their prey with rope? Or are they simply looking to see the longing in their submissive's eyes as they quickly restrain them and tease them from just out of reach?

Once you know the emotional feelings behind you and your partners interest in bondage, you can look at the related physical sensations and type of bondage to use. For example, if a submissive is interested in being terrified and overpowered, intricate rope bondage would not be a good fit—but duct tape would! If the top is interested in having the bottom completely restrained, while having full access to the submissive's genitals, spread eagle on the bed with an under-the-bed restraint system would work well. Is bondage a reward? Silk restraints or cotton rope would work well.

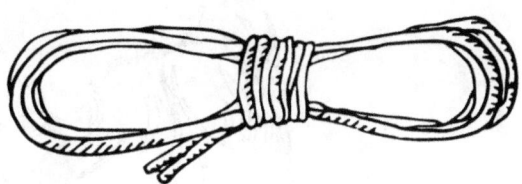

FANTASY VS REALITY

While losing oneself in the fantasy is the goal, all negotiation must be reality-based. As a professional dominatrix, many (many, many) times I have had someone contact me pretending to be a wife who is interested in sending her husband to me to be punished for some misdeed.

While I did occasionally have a wife send her husband to me, and while I would LOVE to punish a naughty husband, I can't properly negotiate with someone who is negotiating from a place of fantasy.

Are they really able to take a long, intense spanking? Or are they fantasizing about being able to take a long, intense spanking when in reality, they're unable to take more than a modest paddling?

Do they really want to have my name tattooed on their ass? Or are they fantasizing about being permanently marked?

Do they really want to get locked in a chastity cage for weeks on end? Or are they fantasizing about it?

Sometimes, we fantasize about things that we can't, or should not, do.

A favorite submissive fantasizes about being mummified and sleeping at the foot of my bed. In reality, he is up several times a night to pee, and neither sleeping in diapers nor waking the Mistress several times a night is part of the fantasy. So we talk about it when we do play, but we both know it's not really going to happen.

Another client loves the idea of being dressed up like a frilly baby girl, complete with diapers and

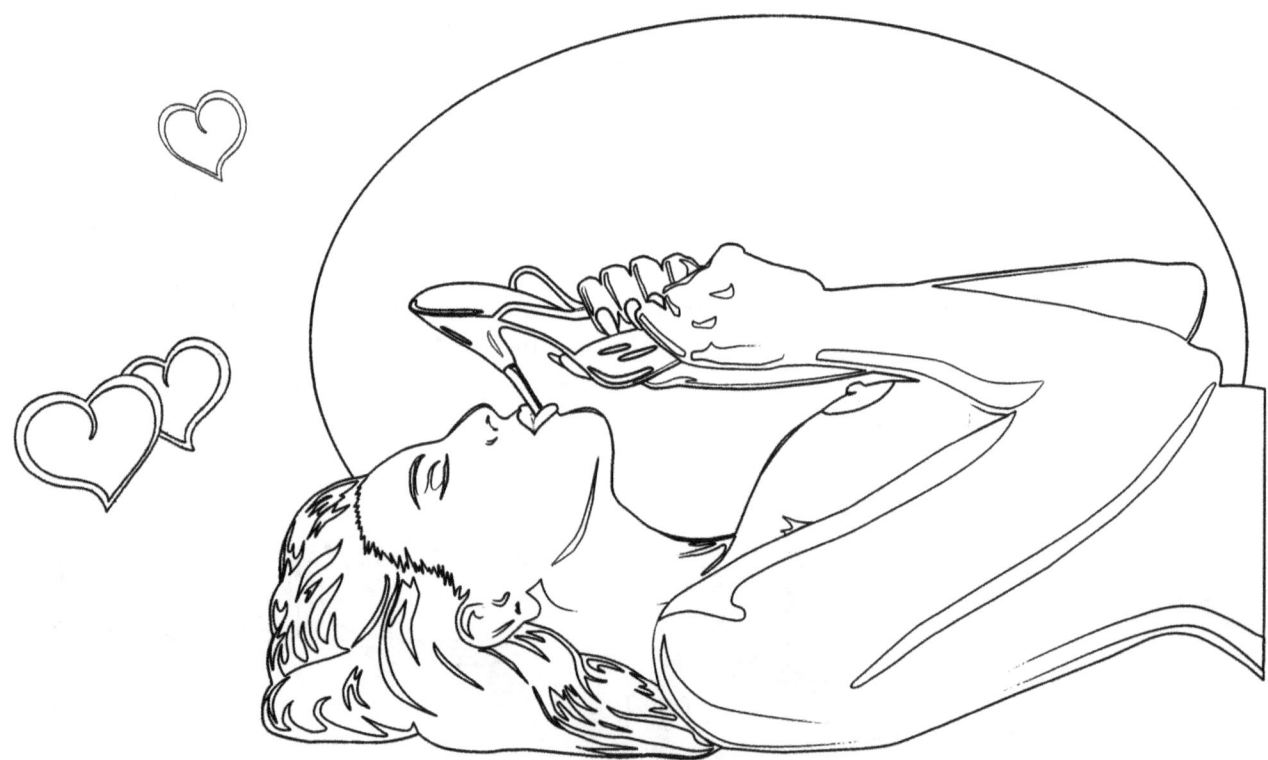

being photographed, blackmailed, and outed to his boss. Obviously, this is not a good idea in real life, but it can be a fun roleplay.

But I also see people who really want to have their bottom marked heavily. Or an experienced chastity client who really does want to be locked away for weeks at a time. Those negotiations take place solidly in reality. I need to know the not-so-sexy details, like does the person wanting a heavy spanking take blood thinners or any other medication that will cause problems? What would the chastity slave do in case of emergency?

Do you need a hint?

Much of kink and BDSM is about finding little things that work and going from there. If you are still trying to figure out the "very important message" puzzle, the first word is AS. This means the "6" goes in the "A" spot in your super sluthing key at top, and in all the spots in the puzzle nwhere you see a 6, you can write A. And 3 goes in the S spot above and you can write "A" above all the 3's below. From there you should be able to figure out the rest of the words and read the message.

And if you just don't get this puzzle, that's totally ok. Just like in kink, you don't need to *get* or enjoy everything.

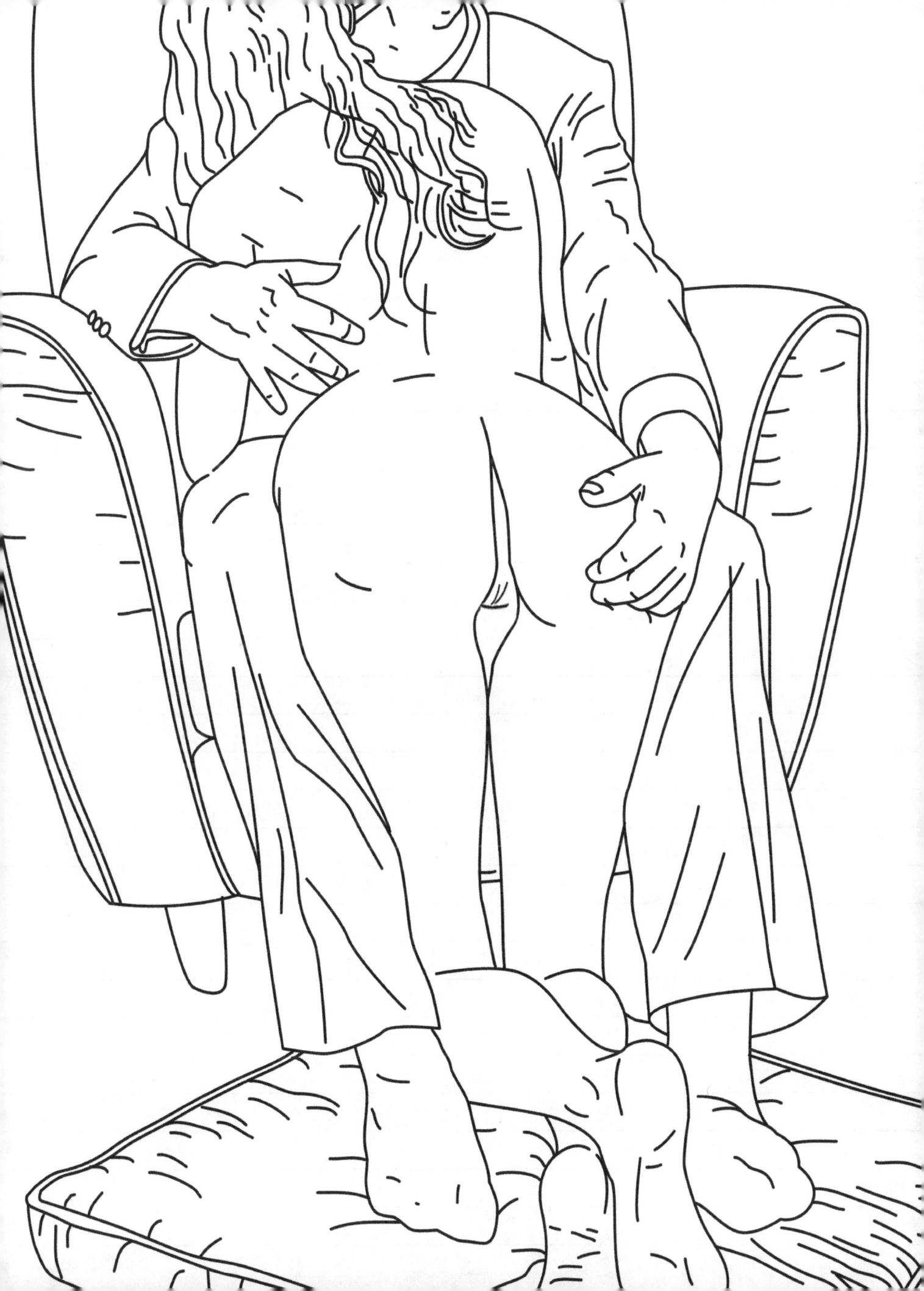

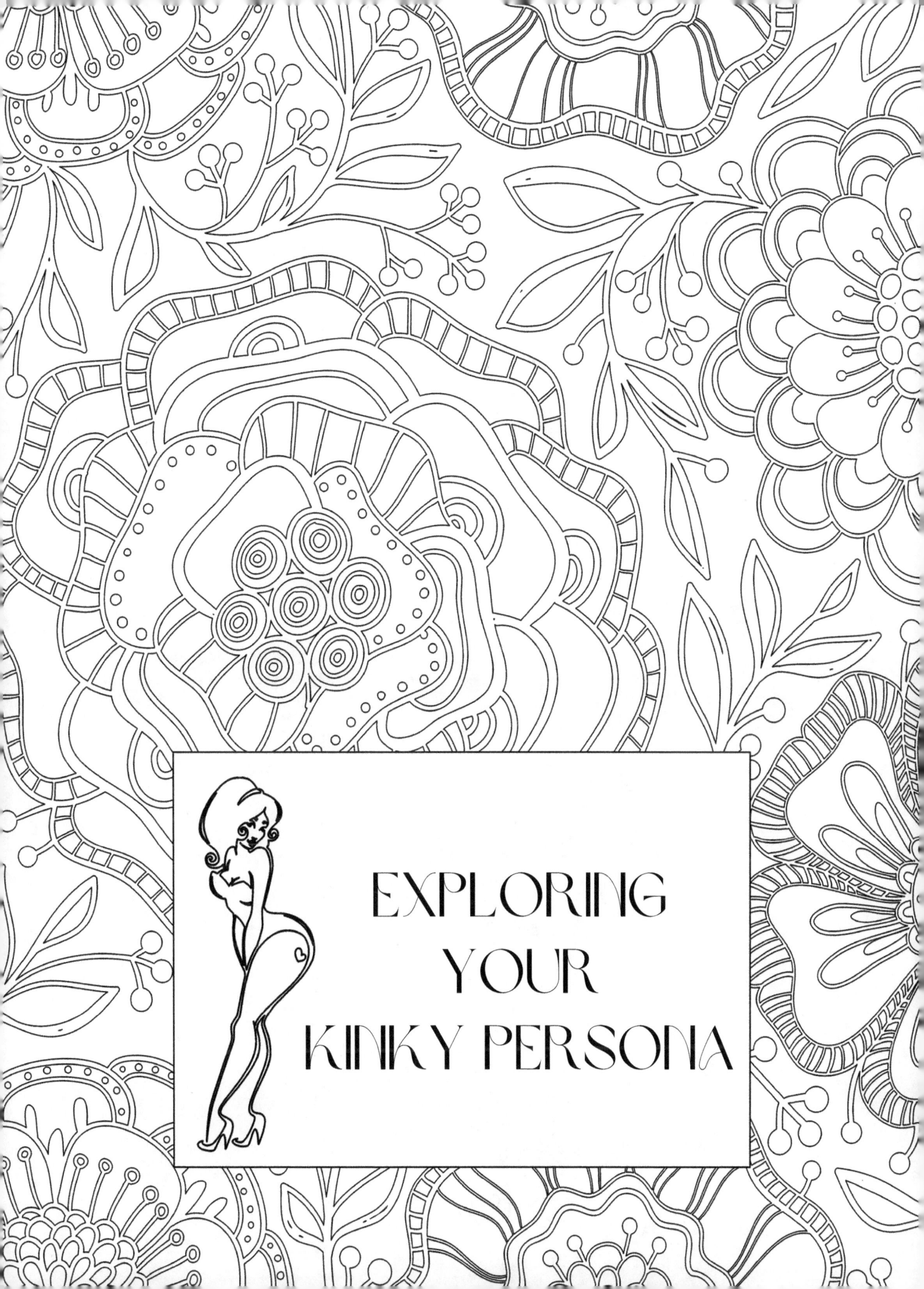

EXPLORING YOUR KINKY PERSONA

WHO ARE YOU?

Kink runs on a spectrum. Some people are completely, absolutely dominant. Others are completely and absolutely submissive. But most people are somewhere in between, sliding fluidly between the two extremes. Certain people, genders, situations, or activities can also bring out your dominant or submissive side.

It's normal to be more submissive when you're starting out—because you're unsure of what exactly to do with your play partner—then find you're more dominant once you gain some experience. Conversely, some people find themselves more dominant when they're starting out because they don't want to give up control. As they gain more experience and learn to create a place of trust, they find themselves more drawn to the submissive role. Others thrive on the constant back-and-forth of power exchange determined only by their mood.

Who you are in kink and BDSM is affected by your past. Have you been in an abusive relationship? Have you had invasive medical procedures? Have you had a really bad BDSM experience? Were you teased about the size of your teeth as a child? The more open you are with these past experiences, and your reaction to them, the more your play partner can understand your reaction to certain experiences when you play.

There is no correct response to any of those events. Invasive medical procedures have sent people scurrying away from any medical play as well as made them fetishize it. Victims of abuse can have anything that reminds them of the abuse on their list of hard limits, never to even be discussed in a sexual manner. Or they can prefer to relive the experience on their own terms, reclaiming that part of their mind, body, or soul. As long as you're open and honest with yourself and your partner, there is no right.

Only what's right for you.

Once you have dissected and discussed your past, it's time to build your future BDSM persona!

Are you a goddess? A princess? A sir? A mistress? A slut? Are you prim and proper? Do you rule with an iron fist? Are you a brat begging to be punished and trained? Does it change, from day to day? Moment to moment? Even when you think you know, as you grow, learn, and experience, it's common to change from top to bottom, from goddess to slut.

WHAT TO WEAR?!

Beautiful fetishwear can be shockingly expensive. I recommend investing in one nice piece. Then supplement with items you find in the lingerie section, at the local thrift store, or in the costume aisle during Halloween. I've also found some amazing things on Etsy.

But! It's not the clothes that make your sexy persona. They're fun to have, but *you* are what makes the play fun. Clothing can contribute to the ritual of getting into dominant or submissive headspace, but YOU make the clothes. The clothes don't make you.

I have done TONS of scenes in my jeans and T-shirts, and I can be just as effective and powerful in those as I can be in my stilettos and leather.

Wear what makes you feel sexy. Yes, I know. You've heard that before. It's rather overused. But it's also true. When I was younger, the tightness of a corset and the way heels made my feet arch made me feel powerful and amazing. Now that I'm older, corsets anger my IBS and heels, while still lovely, don't always make me feel as sexy as they used to. Now silky robes and a fresh pedicure make me feel sexy.

It's not about dressing or looking a certain way. When you're wearing something that makes you feel sexy, even if it's your favorite T-shirt and worn pair of jeans, you radiate self-confidence, and THAT is what's sexy. Dominant, submissive, switch, or totally and completely vanilla, **self-confidence is sexy.**

FASHION

The solution is in the back of the book

Find all the words hidden across, down, diagonally, and occasionally back wards.

```
V I N Y L R A L L O C Z J E W M
E A O T R E N C H C O A T E I K
S M I L E S S E N R A H L N S T
G L I Q U I D L A T E X I A M I
A R P U S H U P B R A S M L R U
R A E C R B M G C L K P E K O S
T R P K R F I L C I M A P L F T
E I C U O R R H R I T I P I I A
R C T T D H A T G H L V L S N C
B O N L G P C I E S C I Q F U A
E C E Y S M E R R Y W I D O W A
L K S L E E H O T T E L I T S U
T R S D H Y T S T E N H S I F C
U I L T H O N G H N C O R S E T
E N L P A W C L I P S T I C K L
A G I M G K V O E G A C K C O C
```

CATSUIT	FISHNETS GARTER	LIQUID LATEX	SMILE
CHAPS	BELT	MERRY WIDOW	STILETTO HEELS
CHOKER	GIMP MASK	MINISKIRT	THONG
COCK CAGE	GIRDLE	PUSHUP BRA	TRENCH COAT
COCK RING	HARNESS	PVC	UNIFORMS
COLLAR	LEATHER	SILK	VINYL
CORSET	LIPSTICK	SLIP	

Another hard truth? Losing weight isn't going to make you sexier. Loving your body makes you sexy. You are the same person at 160 pounds as you are at 200, as you are at 120. The number on the scale has no relation to your sex appeal. Paging our lordess and saint - Lizzo!

Personally, I feel sexier when I can DO things with my body. When I'm stronger. When I'm more flexible. The scale tells me nothing. My triceps tell me everything.

What makes you feel sexy?

WOMEN'S SEXUALITY

Most of us aren't taught about sexual desire growing up and unfortunately learn too much from male partners with questionable intents. We're told that being sexually desirable is a bad thing. We are told that rape or sexual abuse is our fault. How were we dressed? How were we acting? How late was it? Where were we?

Our bodies are viewed as public property, if not to touch then to observe, judge, and comment on. We are told how to improve ourselves—wear this, surgically alter that, starve yourself. It's all about how we look. How we act.

No one cares how we feel. What we want. We are told what we should be interested in—especially about our sexuality.

This leaves women feeling oversexed, undersexed, too fat, too tall, too thin, too boring, too straight, too normal, too wild. We feel like we need to change to be loved. That as soon as we can change this one thing, we will be able to move forward with our lives.

Add sexual desire into this social tire-fire and we can feel hopelessly broken.

A big part of the journey we are on is first moving past that broken feeling. Then, learning to embrace our quirks instead of trying to change them. And finally, moving into our power and enjoying our deviant feelings.

That's why it's so important not to judge other women but to support them, no matter how different they and their interests are from you and yours. We're all on our own amazing journey.

Steps to honoring your sexuality:

- Your fantasies should be valued and given consideration.
- Your body is a temple. You and yours should treat it as such.
- Your desires are important and should be respected.
- Your needs are honorable and should be met.
- Your sexuality is a precious treasure to be treated as such.

HOW TO BE A FEMINIST SUBMISSIVE

One concern I hear often from women is, "how can I be a feminist but still enjoy a little rape play? How can I be a good feminist if I want my partner to use me as a sexual object?"

Because claiming your pleasure and building your life, including your sex life, to suit your desires is feminist. Because men shouldn't be the only ones doing as they sexually please.

Owning your desires and making them happen is one of the most kick-ass feminist things you can do.

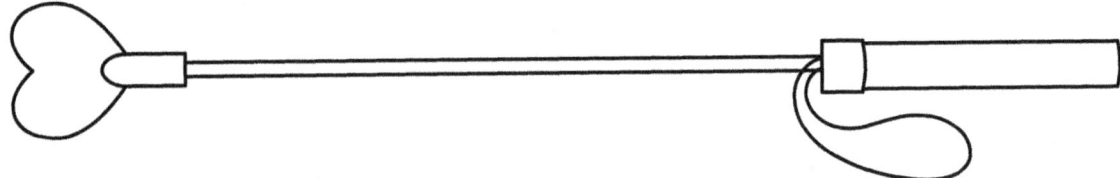

COMMON TYPES OF KINKSTERS

I've created a list of dominant and submissive types. This isn't so you can label yourself, but rather so you can see what is possible. When you're creating your kinky persona, whether you are methodically creating that persona or letting your persona evolve organically, take what you need, leave what you don't. You can fall into one or many categories. You can stay in one category or change categories as you gain experience and discover new activities or interests that you enjoy.

The other reason I wanted to have this list is so that you can see and appreciate what other people might be into. You may not understand masochism, and you are not expected to partake of it if you don't want to. However, it is important to respect other people's interest in being masochists.

You can also build your dominant persona from parts of the submissive subsets, or your submissive persona with dominant tendencies. You can be a dominant fairy goddess who loves to be spanked. It's all about what interests you. Knowing what feels right. Finding out what feels good. And then communicating it to your partner.

TYPES OF BOTTOMS AND SUBMISSIVES

Do-Me Queens and Entitled Fuckloafs

Some people mistake being submissive for being passive and not being responsible for doing any of the work, whether it be physical or mental. There's a difference between not being sure how to react, or of what to do and being a fuckloaf. Those who are just shy or learning will work to be present. Do-me queens and fuckloafs tend to wait for it to be done to them. They rarely give constructive feedback, and often expect their domme to read their mind and know what they like, when realistically, they don't really know themselves because they have been too lazy to put in the work and find out. Don't be a fuckloaf and don't grant them play until they do the work to find out what turns them on and communicate it to you. You are a goddess. Not a mind reader.

Fetishist

Fetishists are driven to their submission as a way to access their fetish. Sometimes they feel guilt about their fetish, and being submissive (i.e., being forced) is the way they receive permission to enjoy their fetish. Sometimes they're not submissive at all. They own their fetish and enjoy indulging in it. Either way is ok as long as there is clear communication.

Masochists

They may or may not be actually submissive, but they find release in accepting pain. These are the bottoms that crave marks, bumps, and bruises to remember your time together. Some enjoy any kind of pain when given with the proper intent ("You are my slave, so I will hurt you in any way that I like"); just one type of pain (for example, someone who is a caning enthusiast); or perhaps just pain on one area of their body (someone who enjoys genital torture). I've had people who've loved spankings and could take any paddle, but flogging on their back did nothing for them. There can be a mental aspect for physical masochists, in that they love the idea that the person they're playing with loves to hurt them, more than they actually enjoy the pain.

SAMs

Smart Ass Masochists! One of my favorites, but not everyone's cup of tea. They want to smart off and see how far they can push you. I love to let them go on for a bit, then take them down. They do need to be watched, because they get such a thrill at pushing your buttons that they can't always take the reality of the consequences. They are sort of like the neighbor kid who teases the dog until the dog finally bites them, and then they're shocked. When they start pushing to where I think their limits might be coming up, I tend to take a little mental left turn on them to shut them up. Example: If I feel their pain limit is coming up and they're still enjoying smarting off, I threaten to put them in a diaper knowing that will either shut them up or start us in a new direction.

Emotional Masochists

Some bottoms crave emotional abuse. They get off on being told they aren't worthy. They are worms, not good enough to lick the bottom of your shoes; cuckolds (men whose wives/girlfriends seek out the sexual company of "real, more capable" men) and sissies (men who enjoy being feminized). They want to feel lucky for every scrap of attention their dominant gives them. Basically, those who seek out a safe place to explore debasement. Especially in a committed relationship, this type of play requires a huge amount of communication and trust so both parties can get lost in the role without losing the human connection with their partner. Aftercare can be especially important with this type of play so that all parties can return to a place of equality afterwards.

Service Submissives

Tea training, butler training, bath assistants, quirky individual obligations like dog walking—service submissives are those who live to serve. These are the ones who love to receive detailed instruction as to how to make your life easier, with the goal of being able to serve perfectly in the background. They want to feel useful, and yes, it can be highly sexual for them.

Sexual Submissives

Some people feel they're submissive because they are sexually submissive. They aren't particularly kinky but like being the bottom in the bedroom. Can reasonably be confused with Do-Me Queens and Fuckloafs, but sexual submissives will put in the work and are more able to communicate their desires and needs, rather than just being available.

Financial Submissive

Money is power, and some people feel a need to give their power, in the form of money and gifts, to others. They get a submissive thrill every time they spend money on their dominant. These people are not sugar daddies or sugar mommas, but people who love to know they are pleasing their dominant with their financial gifts. They are not necessarily in the position to give the kinds of gifts they like to give, but they make it a priority. Some financial submissives like to indulge in blackmail play.

Thrill Seekers

The bungee jumpers of kink! They want to try new things. They want to break a soft limit Every Single Time They Play. They want to be surprised and shocked. They want to do more, take it further, add more people. These intense players can crave edge play in any area that they play in. I include them as their own type because in my experience, these are the submissives who are likely to be open to exploring new areas of kink just to push themselves.

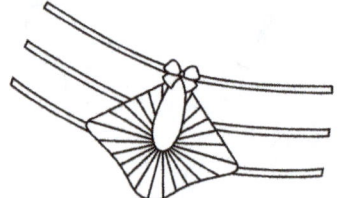

COMMON TYPES OF DOMINANTS

Maternal or Educator

Women who like to take care and educate, even as they hurt and humiliate. They like taking a submissive on their first journey, getting off on the glee and terror of a first-timer exploring their submission. They like educating submissives and showing them the different possibilities and twists available. They enjoy creating submissives in their vision.

Unobtainable Ice Queens

These dominants love rules and have strict boundaries. They make it clear that the submissive is not on their level and they will never be friendly with them. They treat their submissives like a pet or a piece of property, letting them know that they will keep them around as long as they're useful but are in no way emotionally attached and would have no problem disposing of them.

Playful Escapist

Fantasy roleplay specialist, these dominants strive to escape not only the everyday stresses of life, but to escape reality for a bit. They love fantasy roleplay, over-the-top sci-fi, and outfits that may lean a little more toward dramatic cosplay than your typical fetishwear.

Fetishist

While dominant in personality, their main interest is their particular fetish. I've known dominants who only really enjoyed playing with certain types of fetishists, such as foot and stocking, boots, or encasement fetishists. These dominants tend to educate themselves on all aspects of their fetish and can be a treasure trove of information.

Sexual Dominant

Someone who is aggressive in their sex lives, although not particularly kinky. The counterpart to the sexual submissive, this is someone who loves aggressive sex.

Female Supremacist

Women whose only need for men is to tell them they aren't needed. Women who treat men as little more than pets or servants. While I personally view myself as an equal (for the most part!) with my submissives (shhh! Don't tell them!) I love taking little bits that I have learned from my female supremacist friends to add to my pre-play rituals. For example, I always make submissives remove their shoes when they come into the dungeon. Part of that is cleanliness, but part is to immediately put them into the mindset of the shoeless submissive, in contrast to me in my fabulous heels.

ENJOY THE WRONG TURNS

The solution is in the back of the book

Feel free to experiment with your persona. Try on different attitudes. Some ideas won't work and that's OK. Some will work at first, but fail to thrill as you gain experience. Be selfish and choose the approach that you are drawn to, not the one you think is expected of you. It's not about figuring it all out and being done. It's about exploring yourself, constantly, as you change and grow. There is no right. There is only what's right for you.

Financial Dominant

Dominants who take money from willing submissives or "pay pigs." They want to feel that you will enjoy their money more then they will. That you deserve it more then they do. They like being useful in the same way a wallet would be useful. Sometimes it can be as simple as covering a certain bill each month, or more complicated like feeling like they have to give the money up "or else."

Fetish Barbie (or Ken)

Not particularly dominant or kinky, but enjoys showing off their fetishwear. This can cause problems if they attract submissives that expect the dominant to know as much about kink as they do about dressing up. Being a Fetish Barbie or Ken isn't a problem, but not being honest about it is. If you just like to wear the clothes, be honest and say that. No shame.

YOU ARE A SEXY MAGICAL WARRIOR!

Self-talk is self-coaching. When you tell yourself that you are shy, unworthy, unattractive, unskilled, and undesirable, you live up to your expectations. Sometimes it's hard. You feel down. The space between where you are and where you want to be seems like an impassible abyss of suck.

Affirmations may sound corny, but they work. When you tell yourself you are worthy, attractive, witty, skilled, and desirable, you will live up to your expectations.

You can get where you want to go. It may take time. It may not be easy. It will be difficult. But you can either do the work to get there or stay where you are, looking into the distance. This is true for your day-to-day life, and it's true for your sex life. Tell yourself that you are sexy. Love your quirks. Indulge in your kinks. Accept compliments.

I've made a couple affirmations for you to start with, but I encourage you to create your own that speaks to you. Decorate it in a way that makes you happy. Post it where you will see it every day.

Update it as needed. Use more than one if you like.

Dominant Today. Submissive Tomorrow. Amazing Every Damn Day!	Delightfully Twisted
Live Your Kinkiest Dreams!	Feminist Submissive Slut
Be The Kink You Wish To See In The World.	Your Tits Look Amazing In That ATTITUDE!
	My Body. My Life. My Choice.

KINKY ROLES

The solution is in the back of the book

Find all the words hidden across, down, diagonally, and occasionally backwards.

```
T S R N M F U C K T O Y M P O N Y Y T
E S T O Y L P R S D B Y A A E E F D F
R E E S O C Y I S S K X D T A E I D X
O D S R B I P C O E V Q A S S L C A B
B D T E G U P E B U X R M S I C O D E
H O D P N K U Q D I I C E E K U C E V
G G U Y I R P U A P O R P R E W K V I
I S M R P E M E B N T D R T I N T S L
E I M E P T G E F C L E E S O P E I C
N S Y V I S H N U O R V S I E S A L L
Y S S I H A B D K E A E I M I M S L O
S Y S L W M E C G L L P D R T H E Y W
O M E E O S U G S T A E E B L G Y S N
N A C D T C I T T I Z E N Y N L W I L
E I N A C R O I N S S I T E S W K S Z
P D I Z N O L S Y N I N J A E B V S A
I A R Z F I L G S E R I P M A V S Y J
A C P I S U E V A L S E C I V R E S L
L A I P T D K B Y B A B T L U D A Q
```

ADULT BABY	GODDESS	PIRATE	SILLY SISSY
BAD BOSS	ICE QUEEN	PIZZA DELIVERY	SIR
COCKTEASE	LITTLE	PERSON PONY	SISSY MAID
CUCKOLD	MADAME PRESIDENT	PRINCESS	TEST DUMMY
DADDY	MASTER	PUPPY	VAMPIRE
EVIL CLOWN	MISTRESS	RIGGER	WHIPPING BOY
FOOT SLAVE	NOSY NEIGHBOR	SEDUCTRESS	
FUCK TOY	PAINSLUT	SERVICE SLAVE	

THE CYCLE OF PLAY

KINKY CYCLE OF PLAY

In the simplest terms, the kink cycle of play is:

Negotiation.

Negotiation is when you set the size of the playground. You talk about interests, boundaries, soft limits, and hard limits. You talk about health issues (mental and physical) and any concerns you have about the play or the relationship.

Play.

Only you can decide what constitutes play. It can be intense or silly, sexual or nonsexual. It can end with an orgasm, or many orgasms, or someone who is too overstimulated to orgasm.

Aftercare.

Aftercare is ritualized self-care that helps the parties return to their normal.

Following this cycle, each time you play you'll feel safer you'll be able to open up more and trust your partner, and yourself, more.

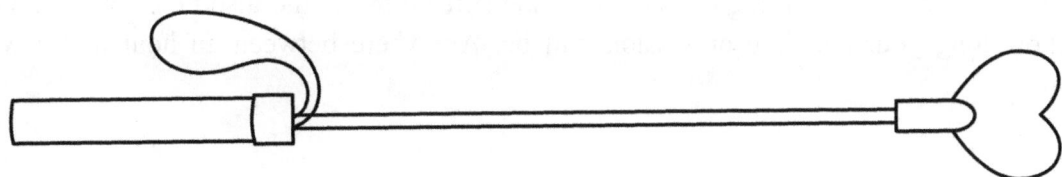

NEGOTIATION

At first, negotiation can feel awkward. Sitting down to talk about what can, won't, and will hopefully happen can feel more like a visit to the doctor than the setup for a sexy adventure. Stick with it. As you get more experienced and understand your interests and limits more, negotiation will start to feel more like foreplay.

While you're still getting to know yourself, formally working through a questionnaire like the one at the back of this book can be helpful. Once you get to know yourself and your partner, you will be able to zero in on the activities and feelings you want. Every once in a while, though, it's good to revisit the questionnaire as people change and grow in their BDSM experience.

Your goal with negotiation is not to create a step-by-step guide to what you're going to do. The goal is to create an arena in which to play. You decide who is going to be the top, the bottom, or how much switching you plan to do. You decide on the feel of the scene and the feelings you want to evoke. You decide on activities and toys you want to use.

Then the top decides which of those pieces they will use and how they want to put those pieces together while respecting the bottom's needs and limits.

By the time play begins, the bottom should have provided the top with all the information they need to use the bottom for their pleasure—spanking, bondage, objectification, etc. The top should have asked for all the information they need to provide a safe space for the bottom to let go and enjoy being used and played with.

A safe space is created when two people trust each other. When neither is worried that the other will violate limits. When neither is worried about their safety, emotionally or physically. When both people know they will not be judged and both people know they are free to speak and ask any questions they might have about interests or fetishes that they don't fully understand.

When negotiating with a new partner, always start with asking how they want to feel emotionally. Do they want to feel owned, taken care of, scared, controlled, silly? Is this all about play and relaxation? Or is there a serious need for emotional release via intense physical sensation?

Then move on to asking how they want to feel physically. Do they like soft sensual touch or intense touch? Thud or sting? Lots of warm-up? To be physically restrained? Tickled? Spanked?

Negotiation should also include time to discuss past experiences in BDSM, past abuse or trauma, what kind of aftercare each of you might need. Hard and soft limits should also be discussed. You should decide how long your playtime or session will be. Anywhere between an hour and a weekend is common.

AFTERCARE

Sometimes BDSM and kink play can be intense. You open up emotionally about fantasies and desires that you're used to keeping secret. Physically, an intense session can be similar to an intense workout. This intensity can leave a person feeling open, raw, or vulnerable. Sometimes these feelings happen immediately afterward; sometimes they don't happen until the next day.

Sometimes they are intense or overwhelming; other times they can just resemble a bit of sadness or melancholy.

With proper aftercare, you might not have those feelings at all. You might feel exhilarated and have a newfound adoration for your partner.

Everyone is different. Every playtime is different. Sometimes without aftercare, you will feel fine; other times even with proper aftercare, you might not. Part of aftercare is simply realizing the need for self-care after you play and the ways in which play might affect you.

The goal of aftercare is to return to your and your partner's normal. Aftercare is meant to remind both partners that what they are and how they are used and objectified in scene is not how you view them in real, day-to-day life.

Yes. You just confessed secret fantasies and desires. In a safe space.

Yes. You just beat your partner. They love you for it.

Yes. Your partner just tied you up and raped you, but only as part of play. Yes. There was name-calling. But there is also respect.

You exfoliate your skin, then moisturize it; the result is softer skin.

Aftercare is like moisturizing your relationship. The result is a stronger, more secure bond.
Snuggles, vanilla sex, a warm bath, a walk outside, talking about normal everyday life, anything that helps you get back to your normal, your status quo, can be considered aftercare.

Food and drink always helps me. Tea, wine, warm snuggles and a snack are my personal favorites.

Sometimes you will find yourself needing more or less aftercare than other times. That's okay. Listen to your body and follow your intuition. You aren't being selfish or silly. These kinds of games require special self-care. During negotiation, always talk to your partner about what kind of aftercare each of you might need. Aftercare is for dominants and submissives.

COMMUNICATION IS NEVER A STRAIGHT LINE

The solution is in the back of the book

You don't always know how to begin. You don't always know where you are going. You sometimes make wrong turns and have to go back. But if you don't try, you will never get better at it, and you will never get what you want.

Sometimes people, especially those conditioned to be feminine, overlook self-care activities like aftercare. We have things to do. People to clean, laundry to fold, worlds to conquer, and errands to run. But overlooking self-care makes it harder to take care of those under you. Taking a few moments to take care of yourself and your relationship before jumping back into the fray will leave you recharged and ready to deal with the day-to-day trials and tribulations that await you.

TOP DROP AND SUB DROP

BDSM is intense, and coming back to earth after an earthshaking play session can be difficult.

You're sharing a part of yourself that you've kept close. You're experiencing huge emotions. You may have been planning the playtime for days or weeks. For a while afterwards, you may feel elated, then suddenly down and depressed. This is called sub or top drop. You're coming down from a huge high. You're realizing you opened up more than you anticipated. You're wondering what the other person thinks of you now. You may feel like you ran a marathon rather than spent a day lounging in bondage.

People experience sub and top drop differently, and some don't experience it at all. Some people experience it immediately, and some don't experience it until a day or two later, which can make it hard to pinpoint why, all of a sudden, you are feeling melancholy.

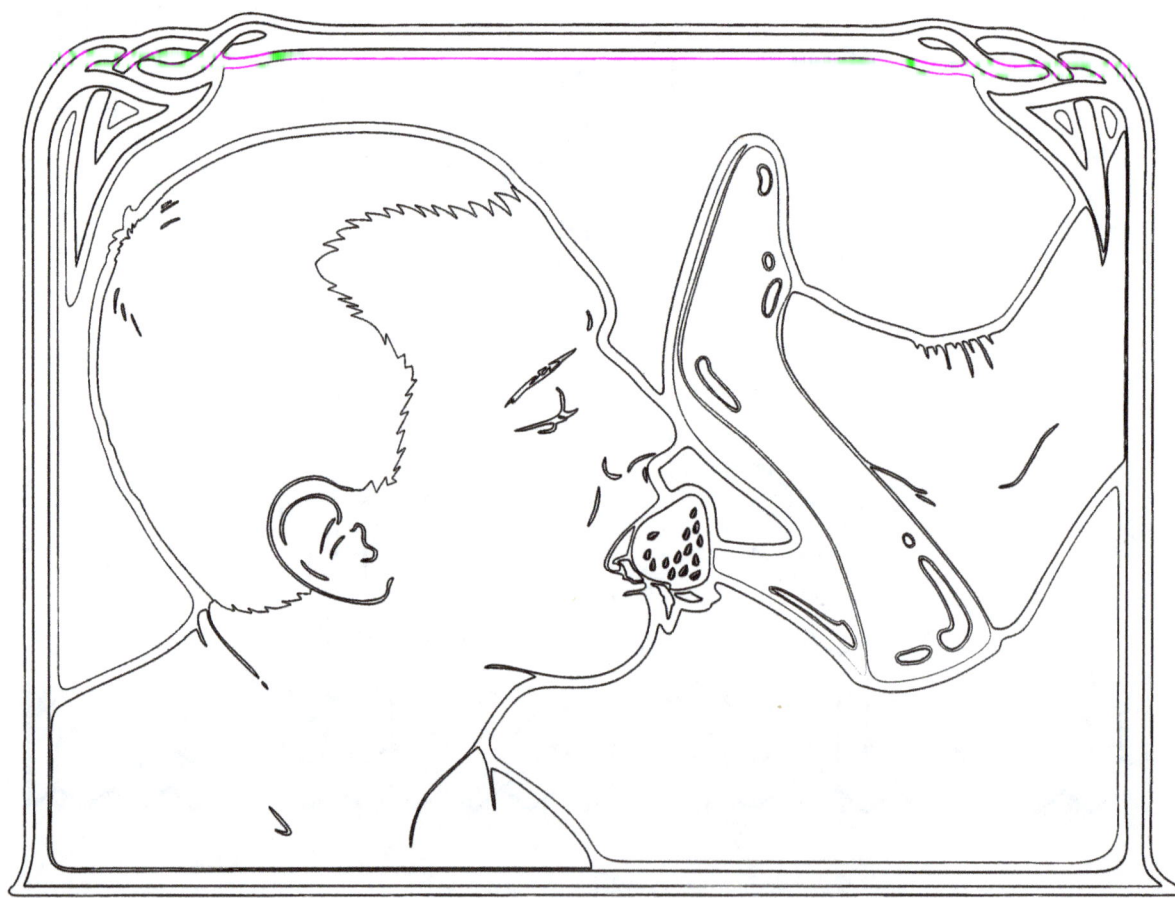

THE CYCLE OF PLAY

The solution is in the back of the book

Enjoying BDSM and kink can take some interpersonal sleuthing. It can be hard to communicate what exactly it is you enjoy about something when you aren't quite sure yourself. Add a second (or third!) person's interests into the mix and it can take several tries before you get it right. And that's okay! Sometimes you will discover something wonderful in your explorations.

Just keep trying different combinations until you find something that works.

Fit each of the words below into the puzzle.

AFTERCARE   HARD LIMITS   SHAME
BOUNDARIES   OWNERSHIP   SNOLLYGUSTER
CEREMONY   PHYSICAL SAFETY   SUB DROP
CONTRACTS   RITUAL   TOP DROP
EXPLORATION   RULES   TRUST BUILDING
FEEDBACK   SELF CARE

The most important thing is to acknowledge it. Talk to you partner about it. Indulge in the self-care your body, mind, and soul are craving. Warm bath. Extra cuddle time. Chocolate and wine. Alone time. Don't put it off. Plan it as part of your play.

This is also a great trust-building time. Simply being able to tell your partner, "I feel sad now because it's over" or "I'm having a case of the post-orgasm shames," and have them listen and acknowledge it is a very powerful trust-building exercise.

KINK AND SHAME

Society giggles when they are uncomfortable, and kink always makes society giggle. We have all grown up feeling like our kinks are the punchline of a joke. The best way to move past shame is to face it head on. Acknowledge it. Talk about it. Shame flourishes in secrecy.

Sometimes, even after you feel like you've beaten that kink-related shame, directly after you orgasm, it can come rushing back as part of sub or top drop. This is normal, and it will pass. With proper aftercare, many people will experience less shame as part of their sub/top drop each time they play.

Occasionally there will be setbacks. Just when you thought you kicked shame to the curb, it rears its ugly head. Setbacks can be caused by a wide variety of outside sources—everything from a stressful family situation, pressure at work, to simply having a lot of time between play sessions. Occasionally, hormonal fluctuations can contribute. The important thing to remember is that it will pass. Talking, snuggling, and coming back to your non-kink status quo is the best way to get past shame. If it continues to be a problem, find a kink-friendly therapist to talk to.

FIND YOUR PEOPLE!

Shame flourishes alone in the dark. Finding people you can talk to who are also kinky or kink-curious can help you realize that you are not alone. Far from it! Even if it's just online, finding your people is invaluable.

If one group doesn't feel comfortable, find another. Each group will have its own feel.

Fetlife.com (Facebook for kinky people) is a good place to start looking online, but also dig around on Twitter using keywords related to your kinky interest.

For local connections, look for munches in your area. Munches are kinky meetups where people get to know each other outside of the dungeon. There isn't any play, and it's a good time to ask questions about the local scene. Attending classes at your local sex shop is also a great way to find others like you!

FEEDBACK AND HURT FEELINGS

Part of negotiation and aftercare should be giving your partner constructive feedback on what worked and what didn't work. Some people feel more comfortable discussing it right then and there during initial aftercare, while still aglow. Others like to wait a day or two to process the play before discussing feedback. Others like to wait and discuss feedback while negotiating the next playtime.

It's easy to take any criticism or negative feedback personally. Just remember, they're talking about their experience. How they received thoughts, ideas, and sensations from you.

Sometimes it can be hard to hear that it wasn't THE MOST AMAZING LIFE-CHANGING THING EVER when you thought you were both having a fabulous time. Remember that it was indeed the most amazing thing ever, and your partner is just telling you how to make it even better.

When you bare your soul and share secrets that you've been harboring, defensiveness can be a natural reaction to any feedback or criticism. Emotions run so deep, and a lifetime of shame can make a simple request or a kind suggestion feel like a dagger to your heart.

But this feedback is important. It can be as hard to give as it can be to hear. If you have spinach in your teeth, would you want your partner to tell you? If your partner really loved when you spanked them over your knee and not so much when you spanked them while they're on their knees, don't you want to know?

This is not a time to be polite. Ms. Manners left the room as soon as the ass-fucking started, so now it's just time be honest.

If you like one touch or activity better than another, speak up!

If your partner says they like one touch or activity better than the other, listen!

WAYS TO MAKE THOSE CONVERSATIONS EASIER

Start with what you liked. Ask for more of that next time. End with what you didn't like. Ask for less of it next time. Or tell them what sensations or activities you would like to try next time to make it work better for you.

"You spank too hard!" may lead your partner to think you don't like spanking, when what you really meant to say was, "I really love when you spank me, but I would like more warm-up."

"You left me tied up too long!" may lead your partner to think you don't like bondage, when what you meant to say might have been, "I love being hogtied, but can we explore more positions so I'm not left in one position as long?"

"You choked me with your dick!" If this was a bad thing: "I love sucking your dick, but I don't like to be choked with it." If this was a good thing: "I love deep-throating your dick, but I need a nonverbal clue to tell you when I need a short break."

SOMETIMES THINGS DON'T WORK OUT

If you tried something and it just didn't work for you, you need to be honest and speak up. You need to be open to hearing that from your partner as well.

"Um, it was okay," is not an appropriate response. It's a response that's going to lead your partner to think they just need to try it again. Differently.

"I tried it. I don't think it's for me," is an appropriate response.

Not everyone is going to like everything.

If it's something your partner is really into, there are ways to come to an agreement.

- They only do it by themselves.
- They only do it with someone else — research ethical non-monogamy.
- Modify it so you both can enjoy it.
- Only do it on special occasions.

The more open and honest you are with their likes, dislikes, and reactions, the easier it will be to trust and explore.

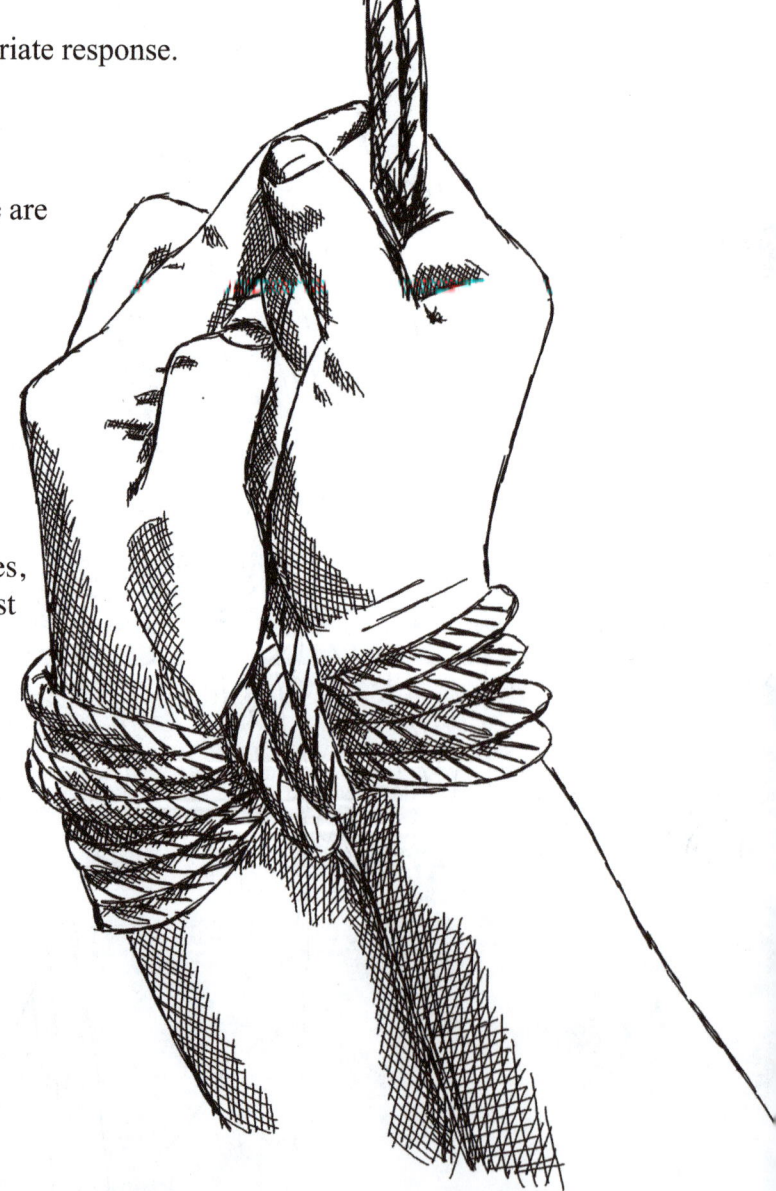

TOYS!

Before we talk about games, let's talk about toys. Quality toys can be expensive. However, some of my favorite toys have come from the hardware store, office supply store, or the kitchen department at Target. I'm always on the lookout for pervertables.

Bag clips, tablecloth weights, and clothespins all make amazing nipple and genital clamps. Test them on your finger first, and watch for sharp edges.

A sheet and a few bungee cords can make a quick, cheap body bag. Plastic wrap is also great for mummification and bondage. Your local packing store will have it, sometimes called stretch wrap or pallet wrap on small handheld reels if you are looking to... pack... in a hurry.

Rulers, wooden spoons, hairbrushes and spatulas make great impact toys.

My toy bag always has multiple pairs of shoelaces for genital bondage. Animal print, black, pink and sparkly, it can be fun to use different ones to fit the mood of the scene.

A door anchor, generally used for TRX or resistance training, makes a great portable overhead restraint point.

THE EQUIPMENT CLOSET

The solution is in the back of the book

Unscramble each of the words below. Each word has a letter that falls in a square. Unscramble those letters to reveal a secret message.

1. TUBT GUPL   1. [_]_ _ _ _ _ _ _
2. AGS KSMA   2. _ _ _ _ _[_]_
3. GIRTASHT TEKCAJ   3. [_]_ _ _ _ _ _ _ _ _ _ _ _ _
4. ARPST NO RSHANSE   4. _ _ _ _ _ [_]_ _ _ _ _ _ _ _
5. REAHELT RIRTATSNSE   5. _ _ _ _ _ _ _ _ _ _ _ _[_]_ _ _
6. WEDNOO PEADLD   6. [_]_ _ _ _ _ _ _ _ _ _
7. NTBAFLEALI GGA   7. _ _ _ _ _ _ _ _[_] _ _ _
8. TAC FO NEIN TALSI   8. _ _ _ _[_] _ _ _ _ _ _ _ _ _
9. FAERS XES SILSEUPP   9. _ _ _ _ _ _ _ _ _ _ _ _ _ _[_]
10. BGYABOD   10. _ _ [_]_ _ _ _
11. FSDNUAFCH   11. _[_]_ _ _ _ _ _ _
12. MEHP OEPR   12. _ _[_]_ _ _ _ _
13. PIENLP SACMLP   13. _ _ _ _[_] _ _ _ _ _ _
14. SOPURTE RLCAOL   14. _ _ _ _[_]_ _ _ _ _ _ _
15. EIBANRMRD   15. _ _ _ _ _ _ _[_]
16. READESRP ABR   16. _ _ _ _[_]_ _ _ _ _
17. NUHAM POYN RESHASN   17. _ _ _ _ _ _ _ _[_] _ _ _ _ _ _ _
18. NOBDEAG BALTE   18. _[_]_ _ _ _ _ _ _ _ _
19. KICFUNG CAINEHM   19. _[_]_ _ _ _ _ _ _ _ _ _ _

_ _ _ _ _ _ _ _ _ _ _ _ _ _ _ _ _ _ _.

[110]

If you're going to do any bondage, you should always have at least one pair of EMT shears or safety scissors around. They are specially shaped scissors with a flat bottom that can easily slide between rope/plastic wrap/duct tape and body parts. They are less than $10 on Amazon.

Once you know your fetish needs better you can invest in quality toys, but never discount the joy of finding pink sparkly bag clips at the office supply store.

GAMES!

This book is here to give you an overview of what's possible to help you discover, embrace, and communicate those interests. The book is here to help you figure out where to begin, in which direction to go, and how to communicate those needs and curiosities.

This is by no means an exhaustive list of BDSM and kinky games, simply a few of my favorites. Each is described in brief detail with a synopsis of emotional and physical feelings evoked. Continue researching the games and activities you enjoy through classes at your local sex toy shop, reading, or online venues such as KinkAcademy.com.

BONDAGE

What

Bondage is the act of physically restraining someone. It can be done with rope, leather restraints, your physical person, plastic wrap, duct tape, scarves or any of a variety of other items. Bondage is only limited by your creativity.

Emotional Feelings

Bondage inspires a very wide range of feelings, from fear and terror to vulnerability and security. Some people feel that bondage frees their mind in a way similar to meditation. Bondage can be part of a kidnapping or punishment roleplay, or part of a meditative "letting go" as the ability to move is taken away. Some people simply love the visual aspect of bondage and don't need it to be entirely secure, while others crave the "click" of a lock, letting them know they are powerless. Tops can enjoy bondage because of the power and control it gives them over their submissive.

Physical Feelings

Some enjoy being exposed, spread wide, stretched. Others enjoy being cocooned and mummified. The feeling or smell of the particular article of bondage may be important as well.

Pro Tip

Types of bondage include beautiful intricate shibari/Japanese rope bondage; predicament bondage, where the bondage bottom risks something if they struggle such as knocking over a bowl of hot candle wax balanced on their chest; and decorative bondage, including breast bondage or using rope to create a strap-on harness.

Use pillows or wedges to help your partner stay in the position you want them, like maybe with their ass raised in the air, or to take pressure off joints.

Use an over-the-door anchor point, like the ones that come with strap type workout sets, to create a quick overhead restraint point.For a super quick and portable bondage kit, have a bottom hold ten coins to the wall. One under each finger. Punish them for letting one fall. Or, see how much sexual stimulation or pain they can take before dropping one.

Safety Tips

Always make sure you have safety or paramedic shears handy to cut play partners out of bondage in case of emergency.

Make sure your play partner has a safety signal in case they can't use their mouth.

Don't bind joints.

Pay attention to feet, fingers and other extremities. If they are cold, or the bondage bottom feels tingling, that's a sign that they aren't getting enough blood circulation. Sometimes a quick adjustment, either of the rope or the position of the bottom, can improve circulation. Other times, removing the affected body part for a quick stretch is required.

Further Reading

Bondage is a HUGE topic, and this is in no way an inclusive how-to. If bondage is your thing, look for books like Shibari You Can Use: *Japanese Rope Bondage and Erotic Macramé* by Lee Harrington or *Two Knotty Boys Back on the Ropes*.

SPANKING

What

Using your hand or other implement to impact your play partner's body. Usually reserved for the buttocks, but also fun on the breasts, thighs, vulva, scrotum, or bottoms of the feet.

Emotional Feelings

Spanking is a versatile addition to any roleplay. A slave being punished will want a little terror. A naughty neighbor may crave humiliation. A naughty girl or boy will want to know they are being paddled for their own good. A mean daddy or mommy might enjoy feeling their submissive wiggle. Other dominants love the ritual and suspense of spanking. There is something delicious about watching a submissive wait, knowing they are about to have a warm, pink bottom!

Physical Feelings

Sharp swats or thudding smacks. Paddles or barehanded. Different implements will have different sensations, so try a wide variety and see what works for you! A cupped hand feels different from a flat hand feels different from a hand with spread fingers. Do they like the physical connection of being over a knee, or the exposure of being restrained with their ass in the air?

Pro Tip

You want to start any spanking with a proper warm-up. It helps mentally and physically prepare your subject. Warm-up is essentially a light spanking. I find it a good time to explore my submissive's bum with my hands, both spanking and massaging their buttocks and maybe pulling them apart. Perhaps this is a good time to slide a butt plug in. With proper warm-up, you'll be able to take your submissive further and spank them longer. You are also less likely to leave marks.

Play with the rhythm. Slow and steady, then fast, then rhythmic. See if your submissive responds more enthusiastically to one style or the other. I also try to use just my fingertips for a lighter spanking, then my whole hand, then maybe just a light rap with my knuckles or the back of my hand. Slowly pick up intensity as you go along.

Warm-up should last a good five or so minutes, long enough to leave their ass a nice pale pink shade. Sometimes when I know the submissive REALLY wants their spanking, I'll make the warm-up last even longer—then make them beg for it.

Safety Tip

Remove any jewelry that could leave unintended marks or cuts. Blood thinners increase the likelihood of marks. A longer warm-up period will reduce the likelihood of marks. Arnica gel will speed healing. As a bottom, if you need more or less, communicate with your top to prevent not having your limits pushed far enough or having them pushed too far. This is a good time to use numbers to check in with each other until you know each other well enough to read their body language.

SENSATION PLAY

What

Using your body or implements to evoke physical feelings. Goes exceptionally well with bondage.

Emotional Feelings

Sensations, depending on what they are, where they are applied, what tool they are applied with, and the intention they are applied with, can inspire a range of emotions: orgasm (vibrations), gleeful laughter (tickling), terror (impact play), humility (spanking for their own good), deep relaxation (flogging).

Physical Feelings

Exposing your body or your partner's body to a wide variety of sensations can heighten their awareness of their body. Being the recipient of sensation for an extended time can make nerves hyperaware and make the brain interpret a wider variety of sensations as sensual or sexual.

Pro Tip

Find different textures to play with. Look for clips in the hardware store, kitchen department, or stationery store with different-size contact points and different strength springs. Add weights to clips. Try adding vibrations to clips. Store sensation items in the freezer or warm them before playing with them to experiment with temperature. Look for muscle warming or cooling cream in the pharmacy to add even more sensations. Most will say not to use on the genitals. Should you decide to try that, and I have, often, start small and use on the thicker skin of the genitals. Not the mucus membranes. Cool water and soap will help remove Tiger Balm or Icy Hot should it prove too intense, but your best bet is to start small.

Safety Tip

Make sure clamps and items you are using for impact don't have sharp edges. When experimenting with textures, heating or cooling cremes, make sure your partner doesn't have allergies to the new item.

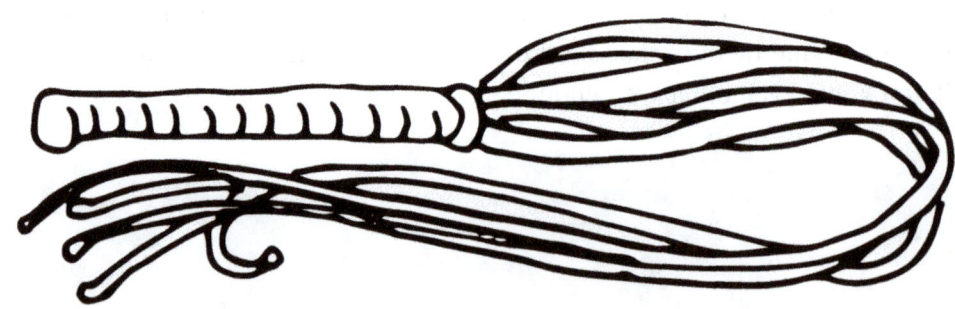

ROLEPLAY

What

Sometimes it's fun and sexy to put on costumes and lose yourself in fantasy, reenact a past event, or invent a new world to conquer together. While many people think of roleplay as secretary and boss or naughty schoolgirl and hot teacher, any roles can be invoked, from strangers in a bar to alien abduction.

Emotional Feelings

Roleplay can be used to inspire a wide range of emotions, so it's especially important to know what the emotional goal is. Terror? Escapism? Humiliation? Laughter? Sexual stimulation? Sometimes dominants can use roleplay to put distance between themselves and their partner to help them step into their dominant role. For example, stepping into the role of Harley Quinn, or other powerful fictional characters, might help a shy dominant feel confident ordering her submissive to do her bidding.

Physical Feelings

Roleplay can be the entirety of the play or just a small part. Sometimes it's easier to dive into kinkier, scarier things when you're pretending to be someone else. If a partner wants more pain than you're comfortable giving, roleplaying a punishment scenario might make it easier. If you want your partner to be more dominant than they usually are, roleplaying as their willful concubine might inspire them to take things further.

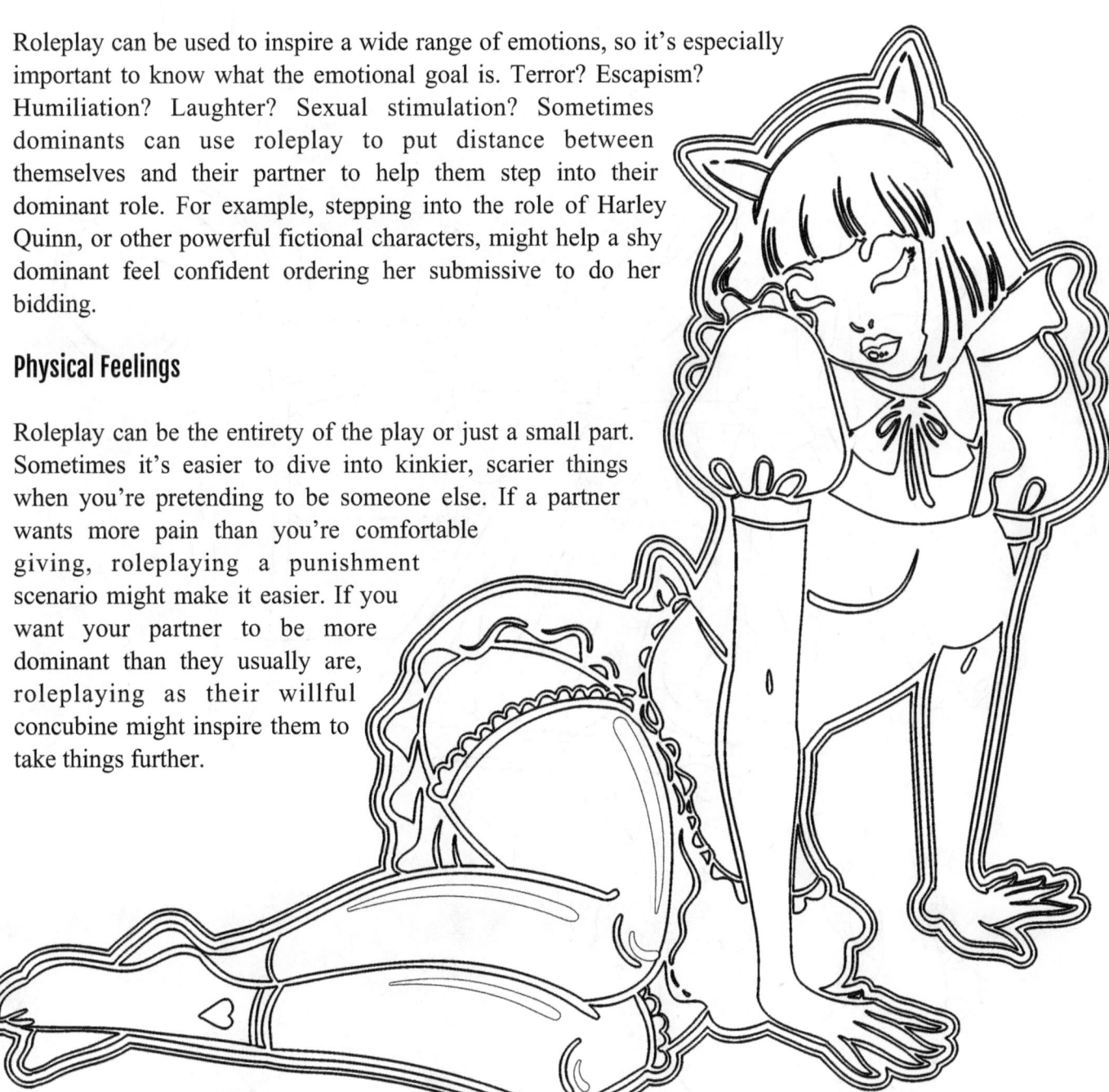

Pro Tip

Even if it's just a wig, putting on your costume helps you get in the mindset. It helps set the mood. It's part of the ritual. Be outrageous. Use a fake accent when you meet your partner in a bar to seduce them. Laugh*. Because yes, it's silly. Have a glass of wine, relax, and get lost in your play. No one is expecting an Oscar nomination. They're hoping to get laid. Costumes help! If you find roleplay is a favorite activity, invest in outfits. There are tons of cheap costumes available online year-round. If you want something more involved and custom, there are lots of amazing artists on Etsy waiting to make your roleplay dreams come true. When you first start roleplaying, plan the start time carefully. Meet somewhere new. A hotel room. A bar. A coffee shop. A professional dungeon. Don't try to go from talking about household or kid stuff to jumping into role. Start the minute you see each other. Even after 20+ years of professional roleplay, nothing kills the creative juices quicker than spending time talking about real life before stepping into my role as hot cheerleader seducing my stuffy professor.

*Always laugh with. Not at.

Safety Tip

Even when it's "just roleplay," it's still important to have a safeword or safety signal! Sometimes roleplay goes into unexpected places, physically and emotionally. Each party needs to have a way to safely pause or stop the play, should they need to.

CROSS-DRESSING AND GENDER PLAY

What

Wearing the clothing, accessories, or attitude of another gender. Generally in BDSM, it's men dressing in women's clothes, but women can have fun dressing as men too! I love to play the role of Daddy.

Emotional Feelings

Some men feel submissive when dressed in women's clothes, following the societal belief that women are the submissive sex. Other men simply like the erotic feeling of wearing their partner's silky panties. Some women enjoy gender-bending and dressing in male clothes on their own, or in reaction to their partner. Most of this information is aimed at men cross-dressing, but many of the principles can easily be adjusted. The reason to explore another gender can be strictly sexual, political, for self-expression, or any combination. Some men love to be dressed in revealing women's clothing and feel objectified by male energy, flipping the script. Others simply like to live out their lesbian fantasies, dressing as a woman and having sex with their female partner.

Physical Feelings

The submissive may want to feel a particular fabric or sensation, or they may want to experience all their favorite BDSM activities from a new perspective. The unbalanced sensation of walking in heels, or having every breath constricted from a corset are wonderful ways to physically remind a plaything of their status.

Pro Tip

If they're giving a blowjob with lots of lipstick on, have them kiss the dick or dildo and appreciate the lip prints. Don't forget to have them reapply their lipstick! Press-on nails can give a submissive an easy way to experience long nails. Make sure they get a chance to experience daily tasks with those nails! To make a submissive feel more lost in their new gender presentation, make sure all five major senses are addressed.

Sight: Mirrors so they can see and appreciate the new look—although some cross-dressers find mirrors distract from their fantasy exposing the reality of the 6'4" bearded fellow in the mirror counteracts the fantasy of 5' busty blonde they've been cultivating in their mind.
Sound: The click of heels, the jingle of jewelry.
Taste: Flavored condoms or lip gloss.
Touch: Silky panties, freshly shaved genitals, sensual lotion, face powder.
Smell: Spritzed in a new scent more appropriate for the new persona.

And in this case, I would include balance. Invest in a pair of heels for some fun themed bondage play. Sometimes simply being told to stand still when you are trying to find your balance in heels is its own special bondage game!

Applying a layer of Chapstick before applying lipstick ensures it won't stain the lips. Moisturize dry skin before applying foundation, to help it apply more evenly. Invest in quality razors and shaving cream if you are going to want a clean-shaven face for these games.

Safety Tip

When a cross-dresser is getting used to walking in heels, make sure there is a wall or something to steady themselves on. Ankle-related cross-dressing injuries are no joke!

Further Reading

If gender play and cross-dressing is more than a passing fancy, I would highly recommend any of Veronica Vera's books on gender expression to help you understand the intricacies of gender play. They are fun and informative.

SERVITUDE

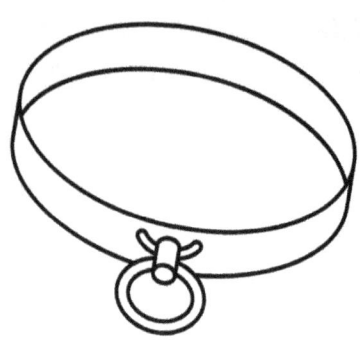

What

Doing chores or other action items to benefit your dominant.

Emotional Feelings

Feeling useful. Humiliation at doing demeaning chores. Pride for selflessly serving. A release from everyday demands by simply following their top's instruction.

Physical Feelings

Sometimes none. Sometimes the weight of a collar around their neck. Sometimes adding limitations that make performing tasks physically difficult, like vacuuming with ankles chained together. Running errands wearing a butt plug. The physical feeling of certain clothing, maid's uniform, or other required outfits.

Pro Tip

Sometimes people like the idea of service but have a hard time with the actual service. Start with small assignments and reward with larger ones. If the smaller assignments are not being completed properly, have a discussion about fantasy versus reality. Is it the idea of service that is intriguing? Or the actual service? If it's a fantasy, treat it as so and don't risk repeatedly disappointing the top by failing to follow through. If the reality of service is the attraction, service submissives can be assigned classes to increase their available skills. If you are interested in being a service submissive, be very honest about what skills and knowledge you can offer.

Safety Tip

Be aware of physical limitations. Service submissives may sometimes be so involved in the job and fear letting their top down that they may fail to speak up when they are doing something beyond their physical limitations, such as yard work in the heat, or lugging a vacuum up and down the stairs.

GAGS

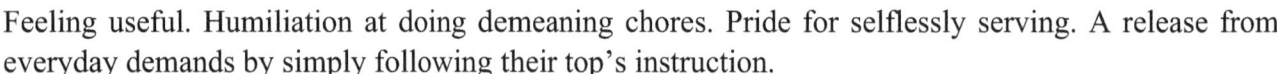

What

Restraining the mouth, sometimes with the intent to muffle the voice. I've included gags under their own heading to provide an example of how a simple toy—in this case, the gag—can be so diverse in the feelings it can arouse, physical and emotional. Many toys can be this versatile with a little creativity.

Emotional Feelings

What is the gag's purpose? To silence? To humiliate? To decorate? To sexualize the mouth?

Physical Feelings

Once you know the purpose of the gag, you can choose the appropriate style. Gags come in a wide variety of styles, shapes, and sizes, and the mouth is a very erotic space, so if gags are of interest, you can gather quite a collection.

Funnel: Human trash can
Play-dough: Age play
Pacifier: Adult baby
Dental gag: Medical play
Fingers: Sensualist
Dirty panties: Slut
Dildo gag: Sissy slut
Used stockings: Foot slave
Ring gag: Hungry slut
Duct tape: Kidnap victim
Clips on the tongue: Masochist
Ball gag: Traditionalist
Rawhide: Puppy
Bit: Pony
Full face hood with built-in gag: Sensory deprivation

Pro Tip

In a pinch, tie a scarf in a knot (or two) to create a quick and easy ball-style gag. The fleshy mound at the base of your thumb (also called the mound of Venus) can make a nice flesh gag. If the left hand is used for the gag, holding the submissive's bottom jaw, the dominant can use their right hand for spanking and exploring the submissive's body. Bondage. Gag. Sensation. All with the flesh. No expensive toys needed.

Safety Tip

The submissive should always have a way to communicate with the dominant when they can't use their mouth. A safety signal such as snapping their fingers works well. People with jaw issues tend to find bit style gags more comfortable than ball gags.

GOLDEN SHOWERS

What
Urinating on or in front of your play partner.

Emotional Feelings

Golden showers can be considered a reward or a punishment. Some submissives view them as a golden nectar to be gifted to them if they behave. Others see receiving golden showers as a sign of ownership with a mix of humiliation and pride. Some submissives may view golden showers as the only taste of their Mistress that they will ever be allowed, or the only way they would be allowed close to their dominant's genitals. The Mistress can enjoy marking her submissive with her scent or gifting the submissive with something warm, intimate, and yet humiliating as her urine.

Physical Feelings

Where on the body would you like to receive it? Or in the mouth? Some equate the feeling of receiving a golden shower to the sensation of being ejaculated on.

Pro Tip

Skip your vitamins 24 hours or so before a golden shower and drink lots of water to dilute the smell and taste. Eat asparagus and drink coffee to make the taste and smell stronger. If the submissive likes the humiliating aspect of being a toilet, telling them to flush when their mouth is full of urine can add an extra layer of humiliation. A submissive drinking a sports bottle full of their dominant's urine when out in public is an excellent way to incorporate public play into your life without possibly exposing others to your play.

Safety tip

Golden showers on the body are relatively safe as long as there aren't any open sores. Any drugs, medications, viruses, or bacteria can be passed from one person to the other via golden shower should they drink it. If you are interested in oral golden showers, informed risk-aware kink also means knowing what medication, vitamins, or recreational drugs your dominant is taking, reading the latest research so you can partake of the activity with full knowledge of the risk you are taking. The body processes and passes on those items at differant rates.

COLOR A COCK

Feel free to customize your cock too!
Cockrings, clips, leashes…?

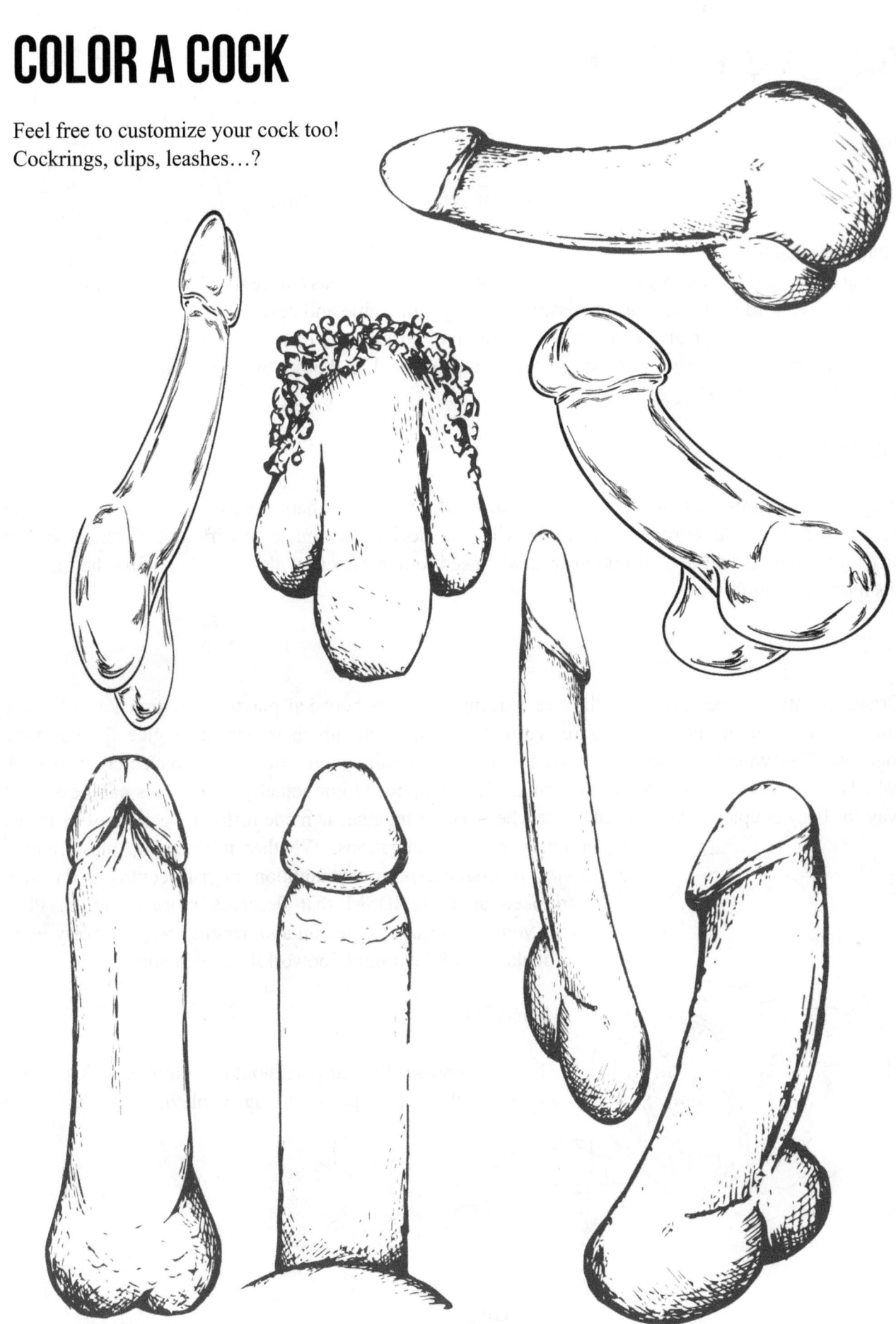

ORGASM CONTROL

What

Controlling the meathod, timing, or frequency of your partner's orgasm.

Emotional Feelings

Giving up control of your orgasm, something you have free and easy access to most of your life, can make a submissive feel very vulnerable and devoted to their top. Ironically, it also makes most submissives obsess over earning their next orgasm. Sometimes orgasm control is the end goal, and other times it's part of the "foreplay" for a bigger scene.

Physical Feelings

While some submissives can be trusted not to break the rules, others should be locked in a chastity device to prevent the temptation to cheat. Chastity devices are made of different materials and in different styles. If you do that option, you will need to experiment with a couple to find the one that fits most (un)comfortably.

Pro Tip

Orgasm control games can keep the fire burning bright in between playtimes. Often I would give clients masturbation schedules before we met to help build up their unbridled glee for our time together. They would be instructed to masturbate for a certain amount of time, or in a certain way each day. They would be told to get to the brink of orgasm, but to not actually come. This can be a great way for busy couples to build excitement when getting together is made difficult because of distance, kids, or other real-life obligations. Whether it's sexting, masturbation schedules, or assigned porn consumption, orgasm control is an often overlooked area of BDSM that deserves more attention. Plus, having your submissive amped up and hanging on your every word makes a girl feel mighty powerful and delicious!

Safety Tip

To keep a prostate healthy, it should be emptied at least once a month through orgasm. If you're playing with a locked chastity device, make sure the submissive has access to a spare key in case of emergency. Numbered plastic locks are available which are designed to be cut off, either by the dominant when the time is right, or by the submissive in the case of emergency.

GENITAL TORMENT

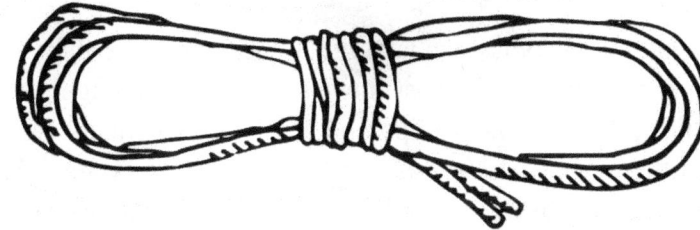

What

Creating a variety of extreme sensations on the genitals.

Emotional Feelings

Genitals are one of the most protected parts of the human body and also one of the largest gatherings of nerves. Allowing someone to have control over the sensations inflicted on them can inspire a great sense of submission. Some people just enjoy more intense feelings, sexual or otherwise, and enjoy more nontraditional touches. The desire for genital torment can also come from an emotional need, such as wanting to feel punished, a castration fantasy, or reliving playground games and being kicked or kneed in the balls.

Physical Feelings

SO MANY! Clips, slaps, pinches, weights, bondage, vibration. Stretching. Compressing. Experiment not only with sensation, but where it is applied. Bondage can be an excellent addition to genital torment.

Pro Tip

A great way to figure out what kind of genital torment your play partner enjoys is to instruct them to put on a masturbation show. Tell them to slap their genitals and see how aggressive they are, as well as how and where they slap. I generally tell them to do it repeatedly to see how far they will take it. Do they get bolder with each slap? Do they shy away? Do they gleefully mix it up with different types of slaps? This also gives them a chance to get past that initial shyness. This is also a good reason to have them prime themselves with a stroking schedule before you play with them.

And of course, you can direct them to do anything else to themselves—tug on their balls or labia, pinch their nipples, etc.—during their show to see how they handle self-inflicting those things so you can have a good starting point in your play.

Dungeon time is a fun and appropriate time to sexualize men in a way they never experience in the outside world. Sometimes subs won't even know what kind of genital torment they can take until you try, although others spend hours at home "researching" on their own.

I always have a shoestring at the ready when I'm playing. Quick. Easy. Disposable if it gets too messy. Add a second one for a longer leash. The possibilities are endless.

Safety Tip

While the testicles can take much more pressure than you'd ever imagine and stretch farther then you ever thought, don't twist them or you risk damaging them. The skin around the genital area is very thin. Always search clips and impact implements for rough or sharp edges. If you are tying your partner's genitals up, as with any bondage, watch for cool skin or color changes as a sign that circulation has been cut off. If you are using shoelaces - remember to keep safety scissors on hand!

Wait. What do I do with that shoelace?

Shoelaces, like clips from the stationery store, are a great, inexpensive, and sometimes adorable BDSM toy. You can get different colors or prints to fit your style or the mood of the scene. And if they get too messy, you can get new ones.

Plus, with a little creativity, they fit every body type. All of them.

To use on penises:

Fold in half, place the center under the testicles and bring one side of the shoelace up around on either side of the testicles and penis, and tie on top. Slowly tighten until it seems tight, then tighten some more. Or at least, that's how I do it. I like to see how far I can push it. Experiment with your partner to see how tight they like it. Once you have done that first tie, be creative.

Go back around again to make it tighter.

Just wrap it around the penis and tie at the top again.

Wrap it just around the testicles and tie underneath the penis.

Bring each end under the testicles, then twist the pieces together until you have an inch or two that is double thickness and bring that up between the testicles, lifting and separating them, before once again separating the two ends and tying them on top of the penis.

Mix. Match. Experiment. Use extra laces for more security. Or use an extra lace as a leash. Have fun!

To use on vulvae:

Tie one shoelace around the waist. Fold the other in half, then secure the middle to the back of the waist shoelace and bring the two ends down between the legs. Tie the dangling ends in a knot so that they knot falls just under the clitoris before bringing the rest of the lace up and securing it to the front of the waist shoelace. Experiment with were the knot falls. This can also be used to secure an anal plug.

A third shoelace can be used, tied to the waist shoelace, brought through the legs on either side of the labia, inner or outer, and once again secured on the other side of the waist shoelace.

This homemade genital restraint can be adjusted to provide deliciously distracting sensations as the submissive walks.

PET PLAY

What

Roleplay in which one person is the pet and the other is the owner or keeper. Pony, puppy, and kitty play are the most common, but any animal or mythical beast is possible.

Emotional Feelings

Roleplaying a pet can give a submissive the feeling of being totally and utterly cared for and adored. Being a pet also gives the submissive permission to grovel at their dominant's feet. Pet play also gives the innate feeling of ownership and objectification. Does your pet want to be shown? Bred? Trained to fetch and play other games? Is your pet naughty and in need of discipline? Or eager to please?

Physical Feelings

The click of the collar, the tug of a leash, the weight of a saddle, the sensation of their tail lightly brushing the back of their thighs. While much of pet play is mental, most pets identify a sensation that helps send them into their proper headspace.

Pro Tip

Watch animal training videos and use those techniques on your human animal. Use a clicker for discreet training in public. Look online to find recipes for making your own pet food and treats if you would like to feed your pet something that fits their role. Have a custom ID tag made for your pet at the local pet store if you would like a little public outing, or online if you would like to keep things more discreet.

Safety Tip

Use knee pads to protect your pet's knees if they will be crawling around on hard floors. Make sure you can easily fit two fingers in between your pet's collar and their neck. If you would like to use a shock collar, use it on the genitals or ankles, not the neck. Electric play should always (with concessions for very experienced players and specialized toys) be done below the waist.

Further Reading

If you are interested in reading more about pet play, look for a copy of *The Human Pony: a handbook for owners, trainers and admirers* by Rebecca Wilcox or *Puppy-Play* by Tosa Alphainu.

EROTIC HUMILIATION

What

Erotic humiliation is embarrassment plus sexual stimulation. I like to think of erotic humiliation as extreme flirting. I've included erotic humiliation as its own game, but in reality, it is usually part of another game.

Emotional Feelings

Shame and embarrassment can be a fun, sexy game when both partners are open about their desires and limits. Bringing erotic humiliation into your relationship can take a lot of communication to understand the difference between what someone finds erotically humiliating and just humiliating. For example, some people find being used as furniture humiliating in an erotic way, while others just find it humiliating. Same with cross-dressing, small penis humiliation, pet training, etc. For many people, just the act of being submissive is erotically humiliating, while others find great pride in being submissive.

Physical Feelings

While much of erotic humiliation is mental, often physical sensations add to the humiliation. The feeling of a diaper being taped on, wearing silky panties, feeling lipstick being applied, being used as a human foot rest, or feeling the ruler lined up next to their cock.

Sometimes physical humiliation IS the goal, such as having degrading words written on their body with sharpie. Even when physical humiliation is the goal, knowing the emotional feelings behind that need for physical humiliation is important.

Pro Tip

Because the interest in erotic humiliation is often tightly wrapped with other games, I like to figure out the other game, then ways to incorporate erotic humiliation. For example, if cross-dressing is the other

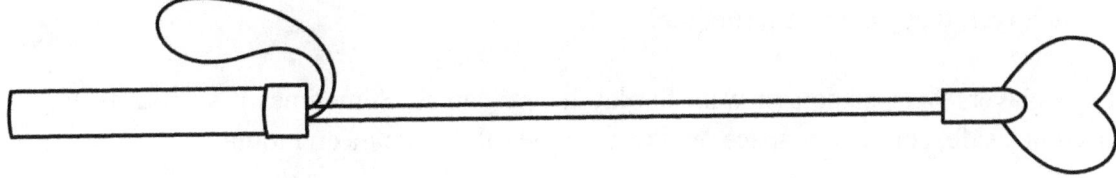

game, rather than dressing them up as my girlfriend, I dress them as a sissy or whore. If spanking is the other game, I like to place emphasis on the pulling down of the pants, or the picking out of the paddle.

Safety Tip

Erotic humiliation can sometimes trigger not-so-erotic feelings. Know what it looks like for your partner to be triggered. Do they cry? Get sullen and quiet? Combative? Do they know when they've been triggered? Some people just suddenly feel "off" and can take some time to identify what went wrong. If you find yourself or your partner feeling like this during the scene, end the scene and head straight into aftercare. Don't worry about spoiling your partner's fun. You've hit a learning point, and with proper care, this can deepen your relationship. Without proper care, it can eat away at your relationship.

Further Reading

If you want to learn more about erotic humiliation, find a copy of *Enough To Make You Blush: Exploring Erotic Humiliation* by Princess Kali.

AGE PLAY

What

Roleplaying another age. Most people who do age play have an age that they enjoy, such as helpless infant, toddler, or teen. With age play, dominants are referred to as caregivers, be they mommies, daddies or aunties. Submissives are referred to as littles. While age play is not enjoying the same pop culture popularity the rest of kink and BDSM is as a result of the "Fifty Shades of Grey" phenomenon, it is widely practiced.

Emotional Feelings

Slipping into the mindset of a helpless baby can feel very freeing. Not only are you helpless but someone is doting on you. A toddler mindset can be more playful, inquisitive, silly, or naughty. A toddler gets punished, but only because the person doing it loves them very much. Some love being preteens and spending a couple hours with no obligation more stressful than coloring in the lines. Those who like to roleplay teens might like to relive the innocence, wonder, and awe of their first sexual experience. Many people who like age play like the aspect of being taken care of and nurtured, or as the caregiver, they enjoy nurturing their little.

Not all age players wear diapers or want to play happy games. Sometimes it's about feeling helpless and abused in a safe, consensual space or taking on the role of the mean mommy.

Some people do age play as a type of humiliation. A boyfriend who has cheated being put in diapers, for example. Those people like the humiliation of being told, and treated like, they are not capable of performing adult activities and so must be shown their place.

Some dominants enjoy the micro-control they have over their little, choosing what they wear, feeding them, controlling their bowel and bladder, as well as their activities.

Physical Feelings

Many age players love a certain sensation or sound—baby powder sifting over genitals, crinkly diapers, the smell of play dough. Some love diapers and have a strong preference toward cloth or disposable.

Pro Tip

Call orgasms a number 3, or a creamy. Use warm pudding to replicate a poopy diaper. Layer diapers to add to your baby's embarrassing waddle.

Safety Tip

People who enjoy age play are NOT pedophiles in hiding. Playing the role of a young person and wearing diapers, or wanting to put someone in diapers, is much different, mentally and physically, from pedophilia. Age play is something that happens between two (or more!) consenting adults as part of kinky play.

Further Reading

Adult Babies: Psychology and Practices: Discovering the structure, motivations and needs of Adult Babies by Michael and Rosalie Bent or *D is for Diaper Humiliation* by Princessa Natasha Strange.

PEGGING AND STRAP-ON GAMES

What

The art of wielding a strap-on dildo.

Emotional Feelings

Wearing a strap-on harness can make a some people feel giddy, but powerful. And sometimes, a little silly. Others feel like they are stepping into their dominance when they put it on.

Receiving a strap-on can make a the bottom feel feminine or submissive. Slutty or humiliated. What is their role in receiving your cock? Is it a gift or a punishment? A little of each?

Physical Feelings

Which hole? Mouth only? Or are they wanting to experience anal penetration, also called "pegging?" Do they want to feel stretched by a large dildo, or is the act of being penetrated enough? Do they like it to be nice and gentle, or do they enjoy being gagged, stuffed, and used? Are they in control as they run their mouth up and down your shaft? Or do they like to be used, with you holding their head or hips and taking control of the motions?

Pro Tip

If mouth only, enjoy being on the giving end. Watch the way they suck your dick and take notes on what they seem to enjoy doing, so you can do it to them later, should that fit into your relationship.

Sometimes the gag reflex is an unwelcome participant, but with patience and practice, your newly minted cocksucker will be able to swallow dick with the best of them. Have them practice relaxing their throat and feeling, but not giving in to, the gag reflex and pushing the cock farther down their throat past their gag reflex. It's often easier to practice on a dildo before practicing on a strap-on.

If they would like to experience pegging, start by using one lubed finger to explore their asshole and anal cavity. As your partner gets turned on, they will start to relax, and you should be able to slip one or even two more fingers in. Try sliding in and out, or slowly twisting. See if you can find their prostate. It's okay to ask for guidance from the bottom as to what feels good to them. Asking doesn't make any less dominant but gives you information for later play.

Safety Tip

Using gloves can not only speed cleanup but also ensures you won't accidentally injure delicate anal skin with your fingernails. Tuck a paper towel or two into the back of your strap-on harness for quick cleanup. If your nails are long, double glove. If your nails are really long, double glove and put a tiny bit of cotton ball in the end of your glove.

Further Reading

Ruby Ryder's pegging101.com

DEEPER INTO ANAL PLAY

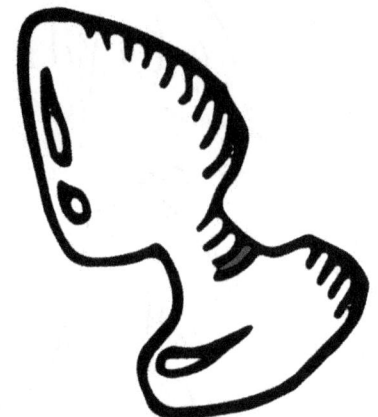

What

Penetrating the anal cavity and/or playing with the prostate.

Emotional Feelings

Having your anus penetrated and played with can evoke feelings of submission, violation, humiliation, or ownership. Anal penetration can make men feel feminine.

Physical Feelings

Some people like to feel like they're being stretched, and others simply like the feeling of being penetrated. Some like the in-and-out motion, while others enjoy the feeling of fullness. Men have a prostate just inside their anus which is highly sensitive and can feel very erotic when stimulated. To find it, slide a well-lubed finger into their anus and bring your finger forward toward their belly about 2 inches. Feel around for something that feels like the flat side of half a walnut.

Kinky Fortune Teller —>

What will your evening hold? Spankings? Bondage? Service? Nipple torment? Only the fortune teller knows! I've filled in a couple of activities, but left four empty triangles for you to fill in with your favorite activities.

Cut on the dotted line and follow the folding directions.

Have your partner pick a color. Spell out the color as you move the fortune teller back and forth (e.g., BLUE—four letters, move 4 times).

Have them pick a number from the inside. Move the fortune teller that many times.

Have them pick a new number. Open the flap of the number they picked to reveal your evening's activities!

Have fun!

Pro Tip

Start small and slow. Use lots of thick lube. The anal sphincter is a muscle, which like other muscles can be trained—in this case, to relax. Start with one finger and work your way up to two, three, or even the whole fist. A set of plugs, small, medium, and large, is great for anal training as you get to know the assholes in your life. If you aren't accustomed to anal play, look for plugs that are tapered, which will make it easier to slowly stretch the opening of the anus. If you are playing with the prostate, experiment with putting pressure on it from both the inside and the outside by pressing on the area between the scrotum and the anus.

Safety Tip

Use non-latex gloves to speed cleanup as well as prevent a sharp fingernail from nicking sensitive anal skin. Thicker lube will work better for anuses. Don't put anything in the anus that is not attached to someone or that doesn't have a flared base. Occasionally there will be a tinge of blood. Usually that's not a problem. The skin of the anus is delicate, and even passing a large stool can cause this. Leave your anus alone for a couple of days to heal and try again.

ENEMAS

What

Introducing a liquid, usually warm water, to the anal cavity. There are two basic types: a small, quick cleansing enema generally used before anal play or pegging, and a larger enema which can involve enema torment, such as being forced to hold it long after the submissive wishes to let it go.

Emotional Feelings

Enemas can be surprisingly emotional! A small cleansing enema can make a sub feel even more submissive, as it's part of their ritual of preparing themselves for their Mistress. A larger enema can be part of age play or a medical roleplay and evoke feelings of being helpless, humiliated, or cared for. Taken further, instructing a bottom to hold their enema longer than is comfortable can lead to feelings of terror and humiliation, which can be very entertaining for the dominant.

Physical Feelings

How full do they want to feel? Ice water will cause cramping. Warm water can be soothing. Using the glycerin soap found in many disposable enema kits will cause the intestines to spasm, leaving them on the toilet for longer.

Pro Tip

If you do a large enema, leave some time for the body to absorb the excess liquid before trying anal or strap-on play. The time will vary from person to person and time to time depending on how hydrated they were when the play began. Do not feel shy about sending a submissive off to clean up. They want you to enjoy them, and a momentary embarrassment is much better than a dirty bottom.

Safety Tip

Don't put anything in the anal cavity or enema that you wouldn't put in your mouth. The thin skin in the anal cavity will absorb any nutrients and other substances quickly. For example, an enema with black coffee will leave the submissive feeling like they drank an equal amount of coffee. Alcohol can be used VERY sparingly, but alcohol poisoning, and yes, death, are possible if you use too much.

PLAY SAFE!

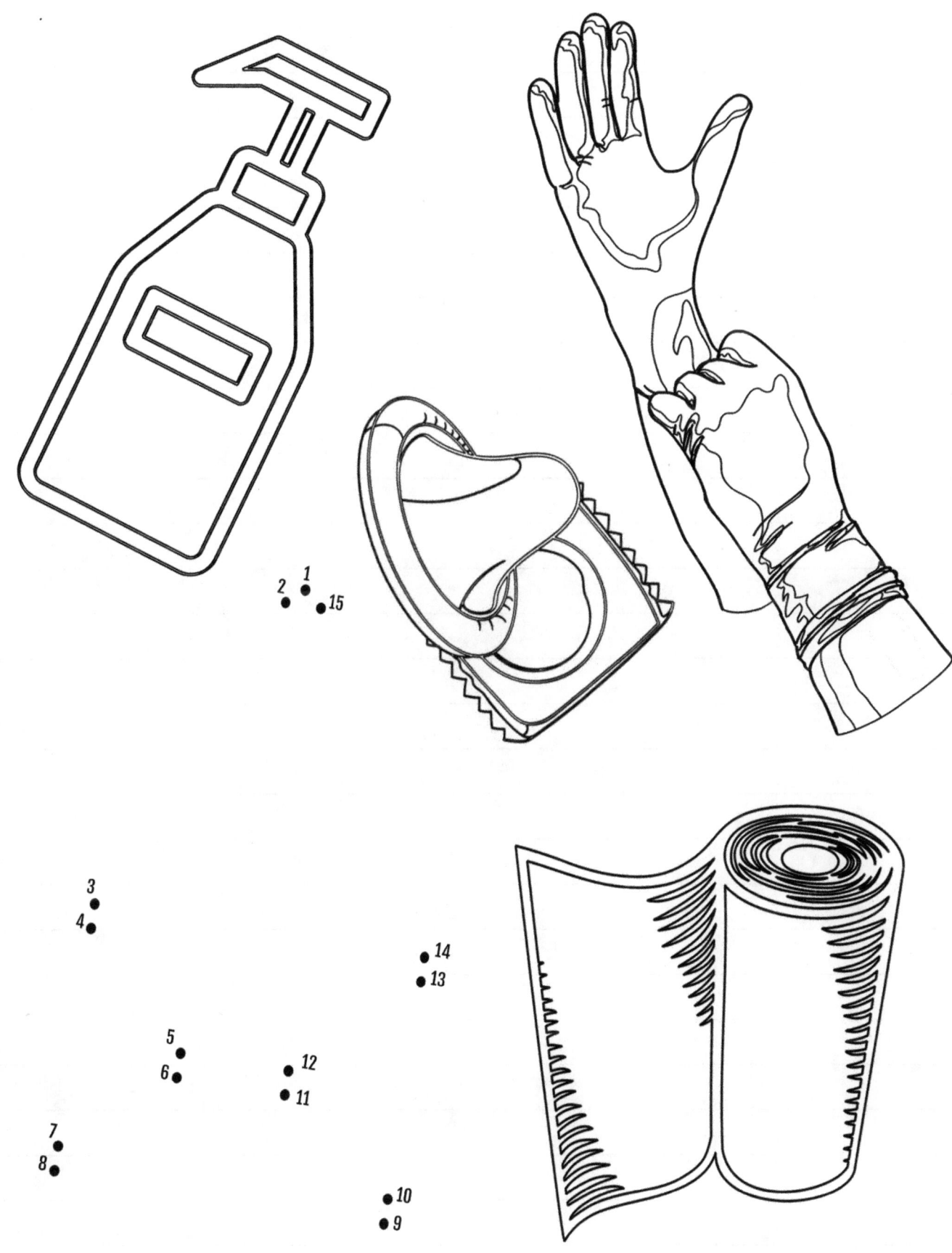

ANATOMY OF A SCENE

BEGINNINGS

How will you set the tone of your playtime? Will the submissive deliver themselves to the dominant at a set time, giving the dominant time to prepare the room and toys to their liking? Will the submissive sit and wait for the dominant after preparing the room, the toys, and themselves for their dominant?

I like to start playtime with a short grounding exercise or ritual. It can be as simple as having my submissive sit at my feet as I have them remind me of limitations, goals, and preferred safewords—not because I don't remember them, but because it gives them a chance to refocus on our time together. Or your ritual can be more involved, such as having your submissive recite something, kissing their collar before you put it on, or performing some other type of duty that fits into your playtime.

These activities and rituals help bridge the gap between the outside world and it's obligations with the escapist world that you're creating for fantasy fulfillment.

- Present the top or dominant with tea
- Present the submissive with their collar
- Lay the submissive's head in the dominant's lap and practice some deep breathing exercises

MIDDLES

Some people prefer to have their playtime planned out. Others prefer to play it by ear and see where things take them. There is no right way. Only what's right for you.

I prefer to leave my plans fairly open. For me, too much planning inevitably leads to the toy I wanted to use not working, the energy not being right, or some other unexpected turn of events leaving me focused on the mishap and not the submissive. I like to have a starting plan, or an end goal, and keep things fairly open.

Whichever way you find works better for you, always have a backup activity in case a toy or mindset isn't working.

ENDINGS

Every scene should end with some sort of aftercare. Like beginnings, endings should be a time to bridge the gap, from the escapist world you have created back into real life.

Think of beginnings and endings as a BDSM portal.

Some of the same rituals can work for beginnings and endings. Laying the submissive's head in the dominant's lap and doing some deep breathing exercises, or the submissive bringing the dominant tea, for example. Incorporate removing the collar if that works for the scene.

Endings are also a very good time for the top to tell the submissive how well they have served them, and for the submissive to thank the top for their time and attentions.

THINGS DON'T ALWAYS GO AS YOU PLANNED

Once you start playing, be prepared to pivot. I've built entire scenes around toys that, once the play started, wouldn't work, and ideas that were just too intense or not what the submissive expected.

Be prepared to let it go and move on to something else. Sometimes that will mean discussing a new plan with your partner before resuming. Other times you can simply pivot on your own, depending on how well you know your play partner and how central the failed event was to the play.

Remember, as the top, it is always your prerogative to change your mind and do something else, within the negotiated limits, of course! Then you can discuss the toy's failure after the play.

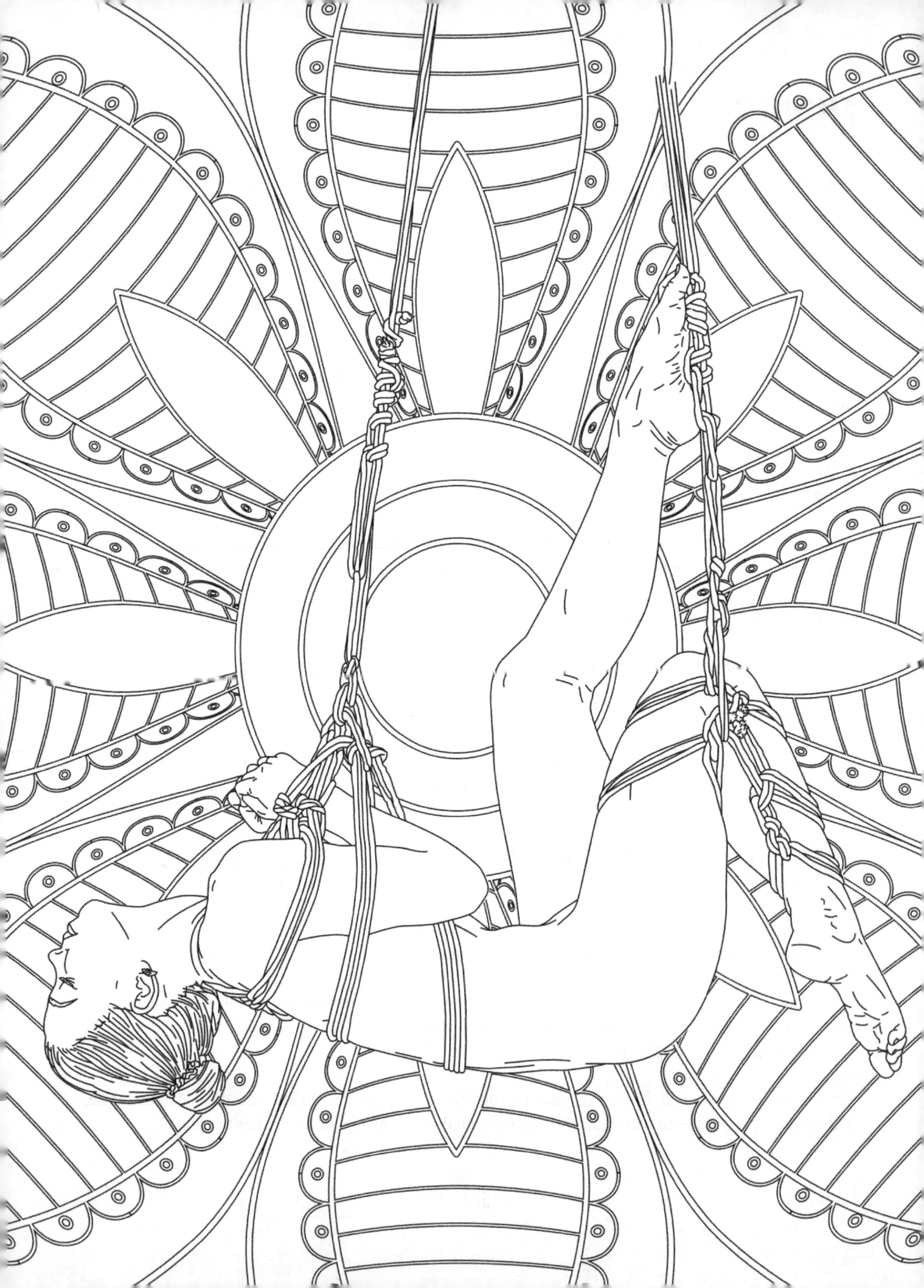

BDSM AND RITUAL

If you're looking for rituals for your BDSM play, look to religion or royalty.

Did you know that no one is ever allowed to turn their back on the Queen of England? They have to back out of the room. I don't know about you, but I think that is a mighty fine rule to have in my dungeon.

Many Orthodox churches require women to wear skirts. Similarly, men in my dungeon are required to wear panties.

Light a candle at the altar? Perfect! Weekly confession? **Yes, please!**

RITUALS TO BEGIN AND END

Ritual is meant to set the mood and help create the mindset of your playtime. Take some time and figure out what you need to get into your headspace. Do you need an afternoon of pampering? A moment to meditate? A certain perfume or item of clothing? Expect these needs to change from time to time, and even from play partner to play partner. Pay attention to those needs. You are NOT being selfish if you need time away from your family to get into headspace. You are NOT being selfish if you only wish to play in a hotel and not in your bedroom. You are NOT being selfish if you feel like you need to buy an item of clothing to be part of your ritual. This is about stepping into YOUR needs. Women in particular end up catering to the needs of others, and sometimes catering to our own needs feels selfish and wrong. Attending to your needs is not being selfish.

Self-care is not selfish.

This may be obvious, but sometimes even the most diligent of us needs a reminder.

A couple of notes about ritual;

- There is no right. There is only what's right for you.
- It can be short and sweet.
- It can be long and involved and complicated.

In order to prevent your play partner from showing up and stomping all over the lovely headspace you have cultivated, you need to be direct and let them know what you expect of them upon arrival or meeting.

This can include what to bring, what to wear, and how to address you.

To also help the submissive get into the proper headspace, I like to mess with their daily ritual. It's a

little way I can insinuate myself into their life even when I'm not around. I like to have them wear something they're only allowed to wear on scene days, or eat something different for breakfast. They have their rituals they take part in every day. By changing that, even in the slightest, you are showing them that today, they are not in control. You are.

It also helps them start to get into bottom space long before they find themselves at your feet.

Once you're both in the proper headspace, it's time to create a ritual around the joining of those spaces. Once again, there is no right answer, only the right answer for you. If you like things formal, create something formal. If you want things on the sexual side, make it more sexual, such as having him be erect when you enter the room. This is how you will set the emotional playing field for the rest of the scene. This is when I let my inner Goddess dictate things. I like to make sure they're aware from the moment they walk in or join me wherever we are that we are NOT equals. Perhaps we are in the outside world, but THIS is not the outside world. This is my world.

HOW TO TURN ANY ROOM INTO A DUNGEON

In my years as a professional dominatrix, I've worked in dungeons that were in swanky high rises, dank medieval basements, lovely Victorians, and more than a couple generic hotel rooms. I've also had a great time with submissives at the local park, the mall, and driving down the highway.

Similar to fetish clothes and toys, having a fancy, dedicated space is nice, but not crucial. A few quick fixes can turn any room into a play room. A good guide is to address the five basic senses.

SIGHT, SOUND, TASTE, TOUCH, SMELL

Sight
Aim for soft, indirect light. Toss a scarf over the bedside lamp, light candles, dim the overhead. If your kid has a nightlight, steal it for a bit. Cheap bedside lights. Camp lights. A string or three of white or red Christmas lights. No overhead lighting! Find a way to display toys. A serving tray full of nipple clamps. An over-the-door hanger holding a flogger. A shower organizer holding dildos. A serving bowl full of safer sex supplies.

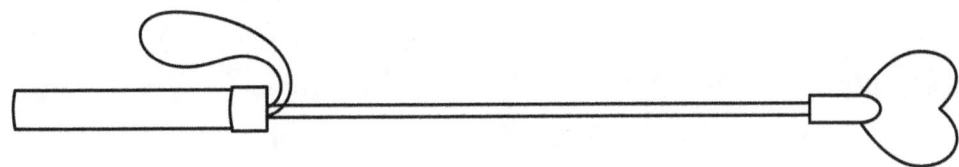

Big Kinky Word Find
The solution is in the back of the book

Find all the words hidden across, down, diagonally, and occasionally backwards.

```
E D Y I C O M M U N I C A T I O N L T F
T U A T O O G Y Y X L C X E R I U A E Y
C N L U W L Y N A A O H E T A O K U A S
E G P L N B M O L S R E S N B O D T S E
E E E S Y N I M P N T E Y E I T P I E V
G O L Y O O N E E U N S K S H D M R A A
A N O T U I D R G G O E N N S L H C N L
D T R R S F E D G C P I O A D O G D S
N N Y I P S U C E L J L K C R N H B D D
O N A D L I C G C E R A H O V E L S E E
B S L H E M K N N S S T W E S S O T N T
A T P D A B W I I K A E R A U N N N I O
A S E D S U U R R B F S E S O Y G I A V
Y I G Y U S K A E A A T P A T E W A L E
N H A P R K M L S T K E E I R Z A R S D
I C C M E P B L I C N L T Y S L L T S W
R O L X I B V O O S N S V I E C K S E K
I S C H U O N C I Z A Q P E N I W E L B
G A W B G F I O I H D E I T G O H R U E
O M U H T M N Y C R E M R O F G E B R V
```

AGE PLAY	DUNGEON	ROLEPLAY	SHIBARI
BEG FOR MERCY	EDGE PLAY	SAFEWORD	COLLARING
BONDAGE	HOGTIED	SUBMISSION	CEREMONY
CHASTITY	KINKY SEX	SUSPENSION	RITUAL
COCKTEASE	MASOCHIST	TEASE AND DENIAL	CONSENT
COMMUNICATION	MINDFUCK	WHIP	MARKS
DEVOTED SLAVE	OWN YOUR PLEASURE	CONTROL	**plus several fun aftercare ideas as hidden bonuses**
DIRTY SLUT	RESTRAINTS	RULES	

[156]

Sound
Music is great for setting the mood. I like something simple that sets the mood, not something I'll find my play partner singing along to at an inopportune moment. Although I've also been known to play "Yakety Sax," so whatever works for you to set your desired mood. Fun Fact: A Portishead CD has been in every single dungeon I've ever been in. Every. Single. One.

Taste
Make sure you have water available. When people get nervous, they breathe heavily. When they breathe heavily they can get sour breath. You're welcome.

Touch
Quickly change the feeling of your bedroom by adding a new comforter or bedcover that you only use for play. Even a simple black or red flat sheet tossed over the bed can add a little dungeon atmosphere.

Smell
The most overlooked sense is scent. Scent is amazing at setting the scene. Think real estate agents baking cookies to make an open house more homey. Whether it's a perfume you wear on date night, an incense or an essential oil you love, find a signature scent to use only during playtime to help transform even your laundry-filled marital bedroom into a sex den.

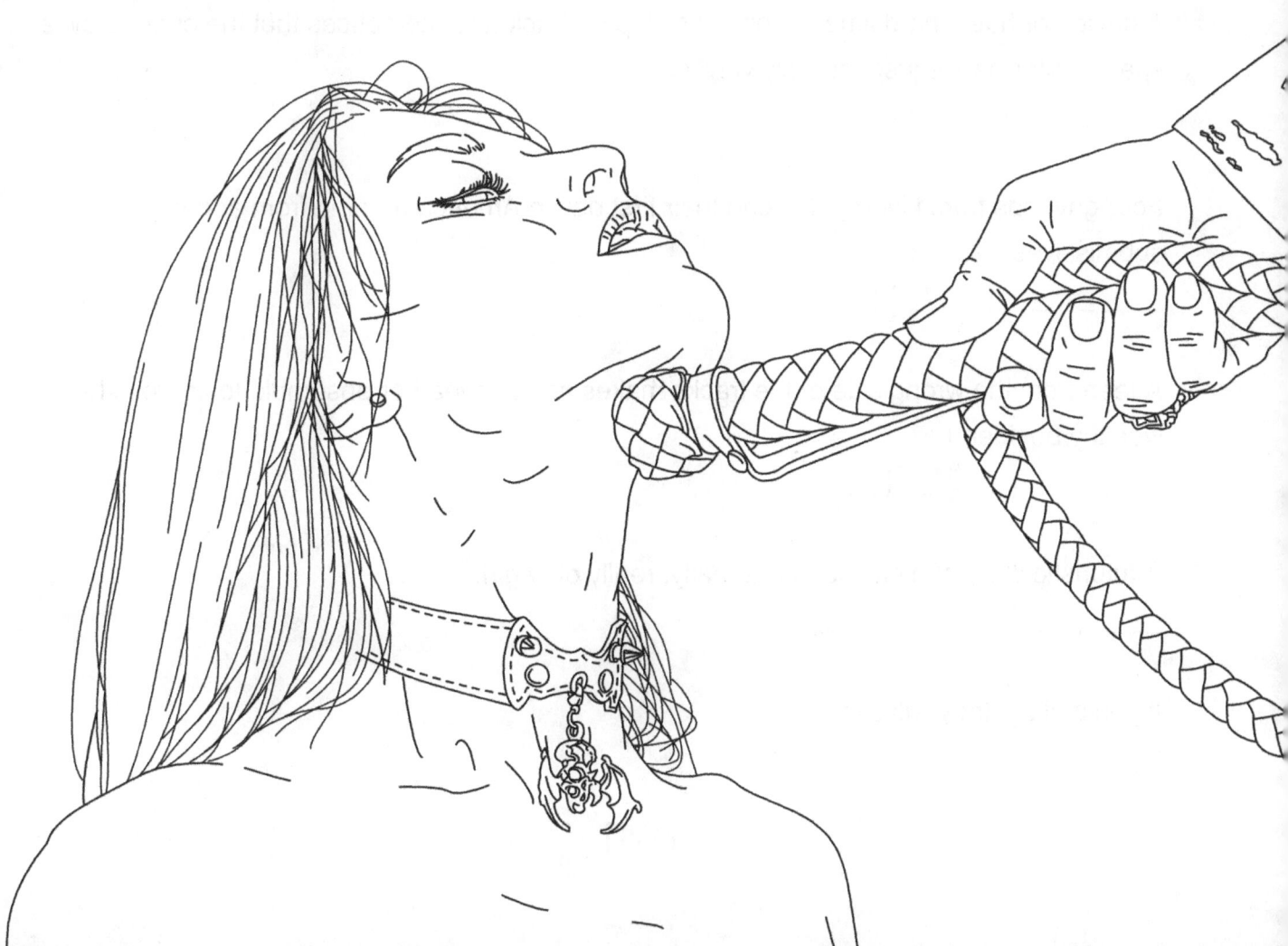

Movie Night!
The solution is in the back of the book

Each of the sentences below describes a pornographic movie that is one letter off a mainstream movie. Fill in the blanks, then unscramble the letters in the boxes to reveal the answer.

(Note: The letter in the box is not necessarily the off letter.)

A tale of a boy toy and his struggles to accept the Mistress's new boy toy.
_ _ _   [_]_ _ _ _

A kinky woman's first date with a vanilla man ends quickly despite his fancy car.
[_]_ _ _ _ _ _ _ _ _ _ _ _ _ _

A princess takes a quick jaunt with a farm boy after he saves her from rodents of unusual size.

_ _[_]_ _ _ _ _   _ _ _ _

A navigator has a hard time keeping his ship on track after he notices that the entire crew's space uniforms are just basically vinyl catsuits.
_ _ _ _   _ _   _ _[_]_ _

Four gay tops from Liverpool spend their first day in America running from adoring submissives.
_   _ _ _ _   _ _ _'_   [_]_ _ _ _

A teen from the wrong side of the tracks makes her own leather ensemble to impress her wealthy boyfriend.
_ _ _ _ _ _   _ _   _ _[_]_

A futuristic story of a cabbie and a really, really dirty girl.
_ _ _   _ _ _ _ _   [_]_ _ _ _ _ _

If you build it, they will cum.
[_]_ _ _ _   _ _   _ _ _ _ _ _

A man's short-lived relationship with a mermaid leaves him with a passion for easy-to-smear foods.

_ _[_]_ _ _

"I'll have what she's having."

_ _ _ _ _ _ _ _ _ _ _ _ _[_]_ _ _

A woman with memory loss trying to find her way home discovers her real home in ropes.

_ _[_]_ _ _ _ _ _ _ _

Archaeologist Jones eternal search for the woman who will peg him properly.

_[_]_ _ _ _ _ _ _ _ _ _ _ _ _ _ _ _ _ _ _ _ _ _ _ _ _ _ _

A bull must coach a team of cuckolds after getting busted drinking the Mistress's bourbon.

_ _ _ _ _ _ _ _ _ _ _ _ _[_]_

While lost at sea, a woman forms an unexpected connection with another woman.

_ _ _ _ _ _ _[_]

A period drama about a high-strung woman discovering the joys of a Hitachi sex toy.

[_]_ _ _ _ _ _ _ _ _ _ _ _ _ _

A wandering dungeon monitor plays two rival submissives against each other in a dungeon torn apart by greed, pride, and revenge.

_ _ _ _[_] _ _ _ _ _ _ _ _ _ _ _ _ _

An FBI agent must go undercover in a golden shower pageant.

[_]_ _ _ _ _ _ _ _ _ _ _ _ _ _ _

_ _ _ _ _ _ X   _ _ _   _ _ _ _ _ _ _ _

> # NICE ASS!
>
> Take a moment to appreciate all the sizes and shapes, and revel in their beauty. Then decorate each one with rope marks, hand prints, and rosy cheeks.

PUSH BOUNDARIES

(Like A Coach, Not Like An Asshole)

Some people like to explore feelings and activities that scare them. Stepping into those scary areas is referred to as pushing boundaries. Boundaries can only be pushed once trust is established and consent is given.

As a dominant, your responsibility is to understand your submissive's boundary and provide a safe place to explore.

As a submissive, your responsibility is to understand your boundaries, be truthful in communicating those boundaries and your interest and concerns in exploring them, trust your dominant to provide a safe place to explore those boundaries, and use your safeword should you need to.

Example: The submissive loves spanking and REALLY wants to experience a spanking intense enough to leave marks.

The dominant's responsibility is to create a space where the bottom feels confident in the dominant's skills and ability to read their body language to understand when to push through a difficult moment, or when to pull back and give them time to catch their breath even if they don't use their safeword. The dominant is responsible for providing aftercare as negotiated (water, snuggles, etc.) and needs to be empathetic enough to understand if there needs to be more or less aftercare.

The submissive's responsibility is to communicate their hopes and fears before play—even the fear of not being able to take as much as their dominant wants to give. During play, they are responsible for being present and aware. They are responsible for enjoying the spanking, but also using their safeword if it gets to be too much.

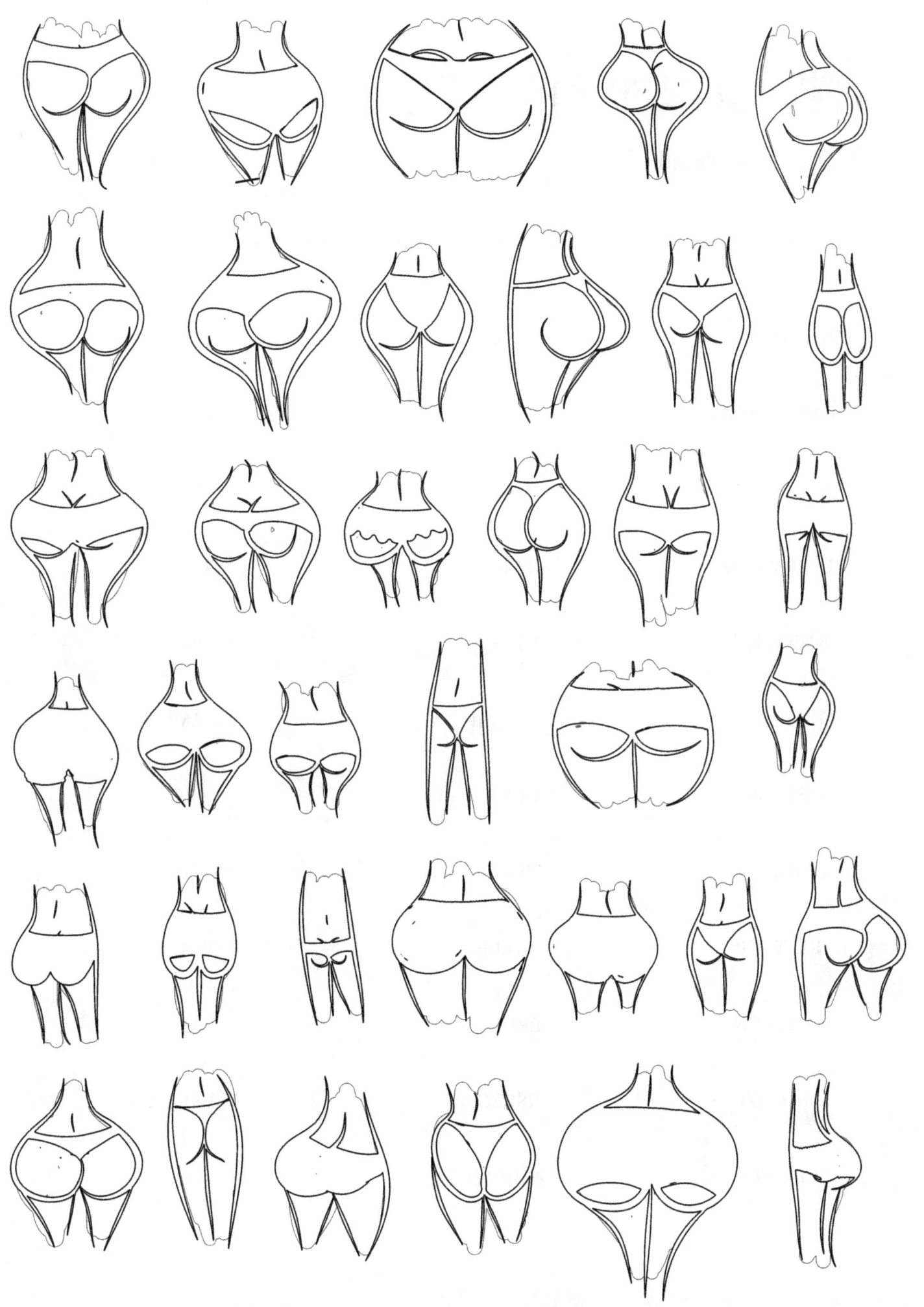

KINKY VOCABULARY TEST!

The solution is in the back of the book

Time to see how much you have learned! Unscramble the kinky words below.

TNIENOOATGI	EFSHIT	TEEAS
FATRREECA	TIISLM	STUTR
ERASELPU	GROMSA	GCAE
ESROWFAD	DPLEAD	FCUK
NNIPKSGA	ILTAUR	APIN
DOPURBS	WTCSHI	LYAP
OPTODRP	UCSFF	EPRO
DEUNNGO	NSKKI	LUTS
RETSECP	NKELE	IWHP
UORINCN	ERLUS	EGB
MBTOOT	NSEEC	ESX
CLLORA	ASHEM	YTO

Contracts, Ownership and Rules

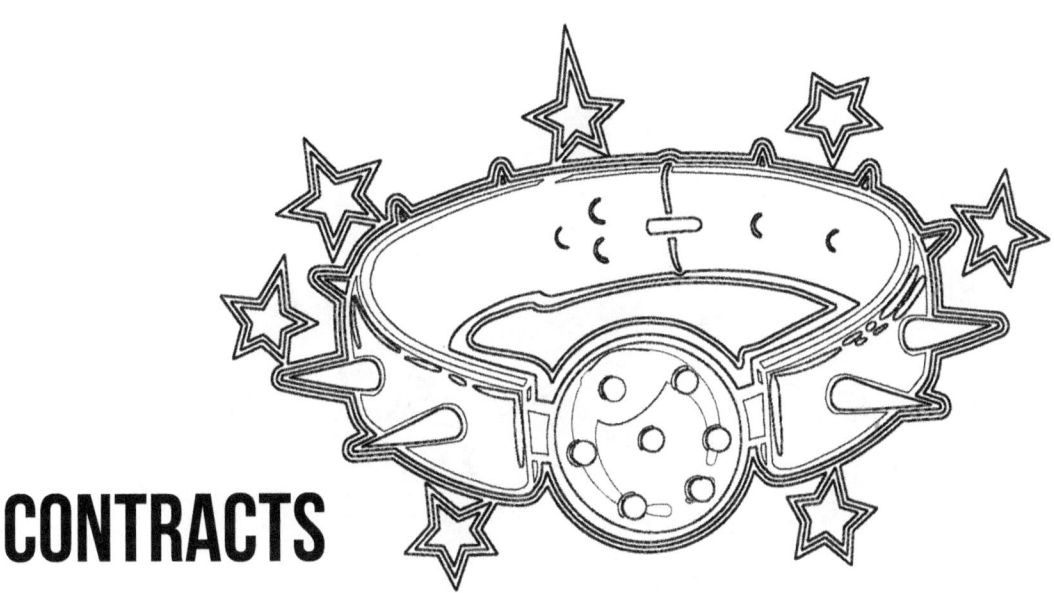

CONTRACTS

Contracts are a fun way to take your Dominant/submissive relationship to a new level. As with all things kinky, there is no right, only what's right for you and your situation. Contracts can be involved, or include only a few rules. They can include only sexual rules or rules that affect many aspects of your lives. The rules are for the submissives, but there are guidelines and expectations set for the dominant as well.

Every contract is individual. The next couple of pages include a template which you can modify to fit your relationship. This is a great time to really examine your needs and your relationship with your play partner as you design your contract.

Take some time to think about what it is you want from this contract. Is it just for fun? To formalize a relationship? To take a relationship further? To spell out obligations? What do you need to reach those goals? Go through each portion once quickly and jot down notes, then again, spending more time on each section to write out your needs and expectations. You can also work through it together, or you can do it on your own to present to the submissive, allowing them to review, request changes, and submit it back to you. There should be mutual respect as well as mutual benefit from the contract.

I purposely don't use the word slave as not everyone is comfortable with the history of that word and there are SO MANY other fun words to use. Pet, kitten, slut, toy, submissive, the list goes on. Use the words you are comfortable with, but also acknowledge the history behind them. Even Mistress and Master have a dark past. But sometimes that's what draws us to them. The taboo.

The same goes for many of the tools and bondage positions we use. Some have a dark history in corporal punishment. You don't need to turn your back on them, but knowing the history can help you be informed about when and were to use those terms, tools, and ideas.

Do you want to walk into a play party full of people of color and introduce yourselves as mistress/master and slave?

ALL PARTIES HAVE INPUT INTO A CONTRACT

The dominant does not make the rules or have the last word. Each rule and aspect of the contract must be agreed to by all parties and based in a place of reality, not fantasy. If you have fantasies of doing something you are terrified of, putting it in a contract is not going to force you follow through. You will still not do it, and then you will have broken your partner's confidence. Or you may do it under duress which is not enthusiastic consent.

A CEREMONY—BIG OR SMALL

Enjoy the ritual of the signing. Invite your kinky friends and have a more formal gathering, or perhaps just a celebratory play party. Or keep it private, sweet, and simple. Either way, acknowledge the step that you are taking with your submissive.

REEVALUATION

Always set an end time, or a reevaluation time. People change and grow. Needs change. Interests shift. These types of contracts need to shift to stay relevant.

Have fun with the contract and write it around your relationship. I've been to collaring ceremonies that were not much kinkier than a housewarming, and I've been to collaring ceremonies that included watching the submissive receive permanent body modifications. I know people who have contracts that make play a priority and book long weekends away from their kids and family to indulge in 24/7 play, and I know people who have contracts yet rarely play because of family and life obligations.

A contract is not reserved for only the serious hardcore players, nor does it guarantee that you will get to play with your partner more. It's simply a fun tool to further communication.

BUT WHAT IF I LIVE WITH MY PLAY PARTNER?

While lots of rules and contracts are well and good for people who don't live together, what about people who live together and have kids and household obligations? Real life can be a buzzkill. If you are submissive to your partner, how do they know when you want to play and when you need your space? If you are dominant, how does your submissive partner know their pleading for attention is part of a fun game and not starting to feel like another household obligation?

By setting up more rules! And, of course, communication!

Set aside time to play. For example, every other Sunday afternoon while the kids are at a friend's house. A monthly meetup at a local hotel. A weekly afternoon at the local dungeon. Find something that fits your lifestyle and your relationship.

If you're interested in having a more fluid agreement, articles of clothing can signify when you are or are not interested in playing. A certain scarf or necklace can mean you're in the mood while a different one can mean you need your space. These physical clues do not replace the need for verbal communication, but supplement it.

While you may not be able to fit in a full-on whipping scene with the kids home, there are ways to incorporate games between playtimes to help fill the void, that won't send your kids straight to therapy. Random rules are great for married couples.

- The top picking out an article of clothing for the submissive every morning.
- The submissive bringing the top their tea or coffee.
- Masturbation assignments while the other parent takes the kids to the park.
- Reading or writing assignments can help fill the void AND offer fun inspiration for when you do actually get to play!

To prevent these rules from becoming simply another obligation of an overextended spouse, set time limits. For example, every day this week the submissive will bring the dominant coffee. At the end of the set time, it should still be fun for both, not feel like an obligation.

DOMINANT/SUBMISSIVE CONTRACT

Temporary Consensual Contract Based On Mutual Respect

Modify for your use. Take what you like. Leave what you don't. These are merely suggestions.

Of my own free will, I, _____, herein known as the _____ (slave name and/or title), hereby grant you, _____, herein known as _____ (Dominant name and title), full ownership, care, and use of both the slave's body and mind as of the _____ day of _____, 20_____, at _____:_____ am / pm _____, until the _____ day of _____, 20_____, at _____:_____ am / pm.

Duration
Duration of the contact. Anywhere between one hour and forever.

Purpose
Detailed purpose of the contract. What makes this relationship different?

- To entertain the Mistress/Master?
- To train the slave?
- To explore together?
- To deepen the relationship?

Collar or Body Manipulation
Does this contract include a collar, necklace, key ring (not kidding!), piercing, scarification, tattoo, or other item that will stand as a symbol for the relationship?

Ownership Responsibility
What is the dominant's responsibility to the submissive? Examples:

- To keep them safe
- To check in periodically
- To spend x amount of hours with slave per month
- To help them explore their fantasies
- To help them discover their true self
- To make them a better person
- To teach them respect
- To teach them to serve

Duties of Servitude
What are the slave's duties and how often do they need to be performed? Suggestions:

- Household duties
- Website or blog maintenance
- Shopping
- Errands
- Litter box cleaning

Personal Duties
Are there any additional physical/emotional needs of the Owner, such as:

- Amusement
- Sexual toy/plaything
- Physical comfort
- Obedience
- Honesty
- Loyalty

Uniform
What should the submissive wear in your presence? What should they wear on a daily basis?

- Panties
- Lipstick
- White buttondown and dark slacks
- Never wear T-shirts
- Cockring
- Chastity cage

Daily/Weekly Duties
Are there any other duties that slave (or Mistress) shall attend to on a daily/weekly/monthly basis that aren't addressed elsewhere in the contract?

Random Rules for your Entertainment

- Bathroom use—must get permission
- Food—a certain thing for breakfast every day
- Must save all nickels to give to their Dominant

Financial aspects
If there are to be financial aspects, list them here. Examples:

- Monthly stipend for Dominant to purchase toys or spa time
- Must ask Dominant permission to make purchases or withdraw amounts over a set limit
- Allowance for submissive

In-Scene Protocol
How shall the Dominant or submissive behave in scene? This is a good place to include any scene ritual. A few examples:

- Remove shoes when entering play space
- Always wear a certain item—panties, collar, ring, lock, etc.
- Leather is reserved for the Dominant

Behavior in public
These can be subtle actions that only the two of you recognize, or something more daring. Examples:

- Always walk on the Dominant's right or left
- Always wear cocking or other item
- Always wait for the Dominant to speak first
- Always take note of how many dogs you see and be prepared to give the Dominant an updated number on command.

Offenses
List out any specific offenses that are particular pet peeves of the Dominant or known weak spots of the submissive. This can be a very individual section, but some examples are:

- Failing to comply with the Dominant's orders
- Incomplete or mix-up assignments
- Keeping the Dominant waiting
- Breaking a contract rule, like wearing leather into the dungeon

Punishments
This can be a tricky one, as one person's punishment is another's reward, but with a little creativity you can think up something appropriately evil.

- Losing playtime
- Caning—for non-masochists
- Writing something out 100 times, a la Bart Simpson
- Losing stroke time or orgasm
- Taking Dominant to the strip club and buying them lap dances, and sitting with their nose to the wall so they can't see.

Training
Could be kink related or not, such as:

- Learning to take more for the Dominant
- Learning massage or other skill to please the Dominant
- Learning a craft to build something for the Dominant
- Learning to properly care for toys and leather

Alcohol and Recreational Drugs
Are there any rules in regard to drugs or liquor?

- Only allowed to indulge on weekends?
- Can never drink top-shelf liquor?
- Can only drink one thing—cosmos, vodka, gin, pink drinks, bad beer?
- Should not drink before meeting you or before play?

Social Contact
What kind of social contact can your play partner have with you outside of the dungeon? These might not be applicable if you live with your play partner.

- When can they call you?
- When/how often can they text? Email?

Sexual Contact
What sexual contact can they have with themselves or others?

- Do they have a masturbation schedule?
- Are they only allowed to orgasm at your feet?
- With a butt plug in?
- Are they allowed to go to sex parties, but only to watch?

Safe Words
Yellow and Red, Chattanooga, Mercy, whatever it is, and whatever it means (stop, slow down, call my mom), document it here.

Aftercare
Owning a sub is like owning any other animal. They need to be taken care of.

- Do they need 30 minutes post play to snuggle at your feet?
- A monthly lunch check-in as equals?

Dominants need aftercare as well.

- Do they need the submissive to bring wine to help them wind down afterward?
- A warm bath?
- A sweet snack?

Signed in blood? Sweat? Tears? Cum? Ink?

SEXUAL ADVENTURE QUESTIONNAIRE!

This chapter contains two copies of negotiation worksheets similar to what I have prospective clients fill out. One set is for you, the other for your partner. Use the worksheets as a jumping-off point. If your partner expresses interest in something that you don't know about, research it. As you learn about it, you may find something else of interest, or a common ground on which to start exploring. If you aren't enjoying yourself, look for something else to explore. BDSM and kink is a huge arena of interest, and sometimes coming at something from a different perspective will help you appreciate it. Reading erotic BDSM stories with your partner can help you explore your interest as well as help you understand your partner's interests in a particular kink.

The most important thing to remember is, don't judge. BDSM is based on trust, and if you laugh at your partner's interest, you have broken that trust. It's okay to not be interested in the same activities, but it's not okay to discount other people's interests. Don't yuck other people's yum. Strive to create a space in which you can both talk about fantasies and sexual interests without shame.

Each set of worksheets can be taken out of the book so you can keep your writing here private.

Each partner can fill theirs out on their own and then get together and compare. Or you can fill one set out together now, and the other set after you have been playing for a while.

This is not a time to be shy and write down what you THINK you should write down. This is the time to share your fetishes, your fantasies, your past experiences, and your future kinky goals.

You may not even know the answers to some questions right now, and that's okay. Go with what you do know.

You may think you want something, but once you try it, decide it was better as a fantasy and decide not to do it again. And that's okay, too.

Sometimes things we didn't think we would like, but we try for our partner, turn out to be a huge turn-on.

Sometimes just seeing our partner turned on by a fetish or activity can change our interest in it.

Interests change. Fetishes evolve. Shame dissolves to reveal more interests.

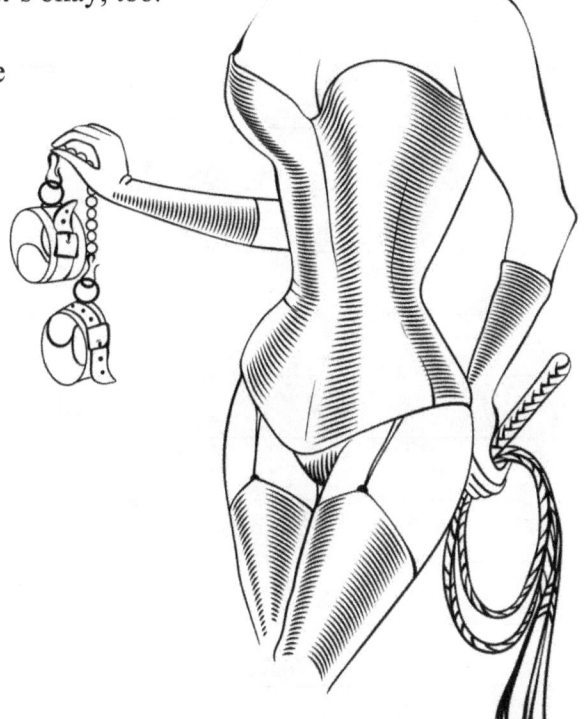

NEGOTIATION WORKSHEET

Now that you have learned the basics, use these questions to help guide you through negotiating your first scene! As you get to know yourself and your interests, you can skip the questions that don't apply and modify the remaining questions to fit your needs.

How do you prefer to be addressed in scene?
This can be a pet name or a regal salutation. Having a scene name can help differentiate playtime from the rest of your life.

What is your experience level?
This is not a time to hold back or to brag. This is a time to be honest about what you have and have not tried, how long you have been playing, etc.

What safeword do you use?
Don't forget to include safety signals if needed!

Are there any parts of your body that are off limits?
If you know each other well, this is might be something you know, but it's important to talk about with new play partners.

Do you have any past abuse I should know about?

Anything that might trigger a bad memory or response?
If you know what it looks like for you to get triggered, let your play partner know. Some people get angry, others withdraw.

Have you ever had a bad BDSM experience?
Something you tried that you didn't like? Have your boundaries been violated? Had a scene go in a bad direction?

Are there any health issues that could affect your play?
If you know each other well, you probably know the answer to this, but it's important to discuss with any potential play partners.

What are your expectations around sexual contact?
What type are you hoping for? What are your limits? How important is orgasm to you during play? How do you orgasm? With a vibrator? G-spot simulation?

What do you hope to achieve by adding BDSM to your relationship?
Sometimes there is an emotional need to be a top or bottom, but other times it's just a fun way to explore each other. Where do your needs fall? It's a spectrum, so sometimes one aspect of play may fall more toward a need, and others may just be fun. You can skip this question if it's a one-time scene, or you can ask what kind of relationship the other person is looking for. Kinky friends with benefits? Life partner? Just stopping by?

What are your biggest fears about bringing BDSM into your relationship?
This isn't necessarily something you need to talk about with casual play partners, but it can be a very scary conversation between established partners just starting off.

How do you feel about marks?
Don't want them? Can't have them? Love them? Scared of them, but curious?

What are your hard limits?
What do you absolutely, under no circumstances, have no interest in trying?

Are there activities that scare you, but you want to try them someday, when the time and energy is right? (soft limits)
These are things that you fantasize about and like to include in your dirty talk or roleplay but aren't sure you could do in real life—yet! A kinky bucket list. What would make you feel comfortable doing these activities?

Is there anything else that you want to talk about that isn't addressed anywhere else in this form?

HOW DO YOU WANT TO FEEL IN SCENE?

Understanding the desired feelings and emotional responses of the parties involved can help set the mood of the scene. Feel free to write in your own!

Circle feelings you especially enjoy. Cross out ones you don't enjoy at all.

Abused	Powerful	Transformed
Adored	Connected	Alluring
Cared for	Ignored	Worshipped
Denied	Neglected	Captivating
Depraved	Objectified	Giggly
Coerced	Overwhelmed	Silly
Intimidated	Teased	Serious
Threatened	Seduced	Controlled
Deprived	Manipulative	Sexually satisfied
Enslaved	Godly	Authoritative
Exhausted	Defenseless	Intimidating
Feminine	Terrorized	Slutty
Masculine	Seductive	Embarrassed
Helpless	Tormented	Loved
Irresistible	Helpful	Humiliated
Bewitching	Violated	Emotionally fulfilled
Dependable	Cherished	Spiritually fulfilled

_____
_____
_____
_____
_____
_____
_____
_____
_____
_____
_____
_____

HOW DO YOU WANT TO BE TOUCHED IN SCENE?

Understanding how your partner likes to be touched can help you feel confident in your approach.

Circle sensations you like, cross out ones you don't like, and draw a line to the body part.

Firmly	WHERE??	Vibrations
Stinging slaps	Scalp/Hair	Lots of warm-up
Snuggled	Nipples	No warm-up
Thudding smacks	Breasts	Pinching
Stretched	Neck	Pulling
Pushed	Stomach	Soft slaps
Tickled	Back	With bare hands
Soft caresses	Buttocks	With implements
Scratches	Legs	
	Feet	
	Mouth	
	Genitals	
	Anus	
	Clitoris	
	G-spot	
	Prostate	

WHERE DO YOU LIKE TO PLAY?

In my comfort zone, please!
A little limit pushing is good.
Let's slip out of this comfort zone and into something more exciting!
It depends on my mood.

GAMES PEOPLE PLAY

Circle anything that looks interesting. Cross out anything that is off limits. Feel free to add your own games and modify as needed! The possibilities are endless.

Lite Bondage
leather restraints, rope, saran wrap, scarves

Restrictive Bondage
leather restraints, rope, suspension

Predicament Bondage
struggling causes restraints to tighten, movement causes pain

Sensory Deprivation or Mummification
saran wrap, duct tape, body bag

Blindfolds

Stocking or Girdle Fetish

Smoking Fetish

Tactile Fetish Play
sweaters, fur, silk, leather, vinyl

Humiliation
erotic, physical, public, verbal, financial, religious, diaper, age, race

Food Play
smashing, forced consumption

Spitting
gifted, on body, in mouth

Forniphilia
Human Furniture

Orgasm Control
chastity, key-holding, forced masturbation, masturbation schedule, tease and denial

Golden Showers
on the body, forced consumption, gifted consumption

Slave Contracts

Forced Feminization, Sissification, or Emasculation

Balloons Play
blowing up, popping, sitting on

Photos/Video
for personal use, for sharing

Boot or Shoe Worship

Breath Play or Smothering

Cages or Confinement

Body Piercing
play, permanent

Interrogation

Medical Play
naughty nurse, catheters, sounds, rectal temperature taking

Roleplay
naughty secretary, bad boss, strangers in a bar, alien abduction

Electrical Play
violet wands, ErosTeks, stun guns

Clothed Woman/Female, Nude Man (CFNM)
Clothed top/nude submissive

Foot or Leg Worship

Puppy or Pony Play

Hot Wax Play

Trampling
barefoot, sneakers, heels, boots

Forced Consumption of Cum

Blackmail

Cuckolding

Anal Play
strap-on, pegging, plugs

Strap-on Worship
mouth only, no anal

Collar and Leash
neck, genitals

Age Play
baby, toddler, maternal, humiliation

Diaper Play
wet, dirty, maternal, humiliation

Over The Knee Spanking

Clothespins and Clamps
mouth, nipples, breasts, genitals

Genital Bondage
lite, extreme

Genital Torture
clips, slapping, weights

Enemas
brief cleansing, large volume, holding

Paddling
wooden, leather, kitchen utensils, belts

Ball Busting
barefoot, heels, sneakers, boots

Nipple and Breast Play
teasing, torture, bondage

Erotic Hypnosis
goal: more submissive, relaxed, slutty, able to take more pain?

Gender Play or Cross-dressing

Service/Maid/Butler Training

Full Hair/Wig And Makeup Transformation
goal: pass on the streets, humiliation, fantasy roleplay

Public Exposure and Exhibitionism
threatened or actual outings

Gags
ball, funnel, bit, dirty panties

Impact Play with Instruments
caning, flogging, singletails, paddles

Physical Impact
punching, hitting, face-slapping

NEGOTIATION WORKSHEET

Now that you have learned the basics, use these questions to help guide you through negotiating your first scene! As you get to know yourself and your interests, you can skip the questions that don't apply and modify the remaining questions to fit your needs.

How do you prefer to be addressed in scene?
This can be a pet name or a regal salutation. Having a scene name can help differentiate playtime from the rest of your life.

_____
_____
_____
_____
_____
_____
_____

What is your experience level?
This is not a time to hold back or to brag. This is a time to be honest about what you have and have not tried, how long you have been playing, etc.

_____
_____
_____
_____
_____
_____
_____
_____
_____
_____
_____
_____

What safeword do you use?
Don't forget to include safety signals if needed!

_____
_____
_____

Are there any parts of your body that are off limits?
If you know each other well, this is might be something you know, but it's important to talk about with new play partners.

Do you have any past abuse I should know about?

Anything that might trigger a bad memory or response?
If you know what it looks like for you to get triggered, let your play partner know. Some people get angry, others withdraw.

Have you ever had a bad BDSM experience?
Something you tried that you didn't like? Have your boundaries been violated? Had a scene go in a bad direction?

_____
_____
_____
_____
_____
_____
_____
_____
_____
_____
_____
_____
_____

Are there any health issues that could affect your play?
If you know each other well, you probably know the answer to this, but it's important to discuss with any potential play partners.

_____
_____
_____
_____
_____
_____
_____
_____
_____
_____

What are your expectations around sexual contact?
What type are you hoping for? What are your limits? How important is orgasm to you during play? How do you orgasm? With a vibrator? G-spot simulation?

_____
_____
_____
_____
_____
_____
_____
_____
_____
_____
_____

What do you hope to achieve by adding BDSM to your relationship?
Sometimes there is an emotional need to be a top or bottom, but other times it's just a fun way to explore each other. Where do your needs fall? It's a spectrum, so sometimes one aspect of play may fall more toward a need, and others may just be fun. You can skip this question if it's a one-time scene, or you can ask what kind of relationship the other person is looking for. Kinky friends with benefits? Life partner? Just stopping by?

What are your biggest fears about bringing BDSM into your relationship?
This isn't necessarily something you need to talk about with casual play partners, but it can be a very scary conversation between established partners just starting off.

How do you feel about marks?
Don't want them? Can't have them? Love them? Scared of them, but curious?

What are your hard limits?
What do you absolutely, under no circumstances, have no interest in trying?

Are there activities that scare you, but you want to try them someday, when the time and energy is right? (soft limits)

These are things that you fantasize about and like to include in your dirty talk or roleplay but aren't sure you could do in real life—yet! A kinky bucket list. What would make you feel comfortable doing these activities?

Is there anything else that you want to talk about that isn't addressed anywhere else in this form?

HOW DO YOU WANT TO FEEL IN SCENE?

Understanding the desired feelings and emotional responses of the parties involved can help set the mood of the scene. Feel free to write in your own!

Circle feelings you especially enjoy. Cross out ones you don't enjoy at all.

Abused	Powerful	Transformed
Adored	Connected	Alluring
Cared for	Ignored	Worshipped
Denied	Neglected	Captivating
Depraved	Objectified	Giggly
Coerced	Overwhelmed	Silly
Intimidated	Teased	Serious
Threatened	Seduced	Controlled
Deprived	Manipulative	Sexually satisfied
Enslaved	Godly	Authoritative
Exhausted	Defenseless	Intimidating
Feminine	Terrorized	Slutty
Masculine	Seductive	Embarrassed
Helpless	Tormented	Loved
Irresistible	Helpful	Humiliated
Bewitching	Violated	Emotionally fulfilled
Dependable	Cherished	Spiritually fulfilled

HOW DO YOU WANT TO BE TOUCHED IN SCENE?

Understanding how your partner likes to be touched can help you feel confident in your approach.

Circle sensations you like, cross out ones you don't like, and draw a line to the body part.

Firmly	WHERE??	Vibrations
Stinging slaps	Scalp/Hair	Lots of warm-up
Snuggled	Nipples	No warm-up
Thudding smacks	Breasts	Pinching
Stretched	Neck	Pulling
Pushed	Stomach	Soft slaps
Tickled	Back	With bare hands
Soft caresses	Buttocks	With implements
Scratches	Legs	
	Feet	
	Mouth	
	Genitals	
	Anus	
	Clitoris	
	G-spot	
	Prostate	

_____
_____
_____
_____
_____
_____

WHERE DO YOU LIKE TO PLAY?

In my comfort zone, please!
A little limit pushing is good.
Let's slip out of this comfort zone and into something more exciting!
It depends on my mood.

_____
_____
_____
_____

GAMES PEOPLE PLAY

Circle anything that looks interesting. Cross out anything that is off limits. Feel free to add your own games and modify as needed! The possibilities are endless.

Lite Bondage
leather restraints, rope, saran wrap, scarves

Restrictive Bondage
leather restraints, rope, suspension

Predicament Bondage
stuggling causes restraints to tighten, movement causes pain

Sensory Deprivation or Mummification
saran wrap, duct tape, body bag

Blindfolds

Stocking or Girdle Fetish

Smoking Fetish

Tactile Fetish Play
sweaters, fur, silk, leather, vinyl

Humiliation
erotic, physical, public, verbal, financial, religious, diaper, age, race

Food Play
smashing, forced consumption

Spitting
gifted, on body, in mouth

Forniphilia
Human Furniture

Orgasm Control
chastity, key-holding, forced masturbation, masturbation schedule, tease and denial

Golden Showers
on the body, forced consumption, gifted consumption

Slave Contracts

Forced Feminization, Sissification, or Emasculation

Balloons Play
blowing up, popping, sitting on

Photos/Video
for personal use, for sharing

Boot or Shoe Worship

Breath Play or Smothering

Cages or Confinement

Body Piercing
play, permanent

Interrogation

Medical Play
naughty nurse, catheters, sounds, rectal temperature taking

Role-play
naughty secretary, bad boss, strangers in a bar, alien abduction

Electrical Play
violet wands, ErosTeks, stun guns

Clothed Woman/Female, Nude Man
Clothed top/ nude submissive

Foot or Leg Worship

Puppy or Pony Play

Hot Wax Play

Trampling
barefoot, sneakers, heels, boots

Forced Consumption of Cum

Blackmail

Cuckolding

Anal Play
strap-on, pegging, plugs

Strap-on Worship
mouth only, no anal

Collar and Leash
neck, genitals

Age Play
baby, toddler, maternal, humiliation

Diaper Play
wet, dirty, maternal, humiliation

Over The Knee Spanking

Clothespins and Clamps
mouth, nipples, breasts, genitals

Genital Bondage
lite, extreme

Genital Torture
clips, slapping, weights

Enemas
brief cleansing, large volume, holding

Paddling
wooden, leather, kitchen utensils, belts

Ball Busting
barefoot, heels, sneakers, boots

Nipple and Breast Play
teasing, torture, bondage

Erotic Hypnosis
goal: more submissive, relaxed, slutty, able to take more pain?

Gender Play or Crossdressing

Service/Maid/Butler Training

Full Hair/Wig And Makeup Transformation
goal: pass on the streets, humiliation, fantasy roleplay

Public Exposure and Exhibitionism
threatened or actual outings

Gags
ball, funnel, bit, dirty panties

Impact Play with Instruments
caning, flogging, singletails, paddles

Physical Impact
punching, hitting, face-slapping

FEELING LOST

page 22

RISK AWARE CONSENSUAL KINK

page 30

SAFEWORDS

page 28

Thank you Mistress,
May I have another?

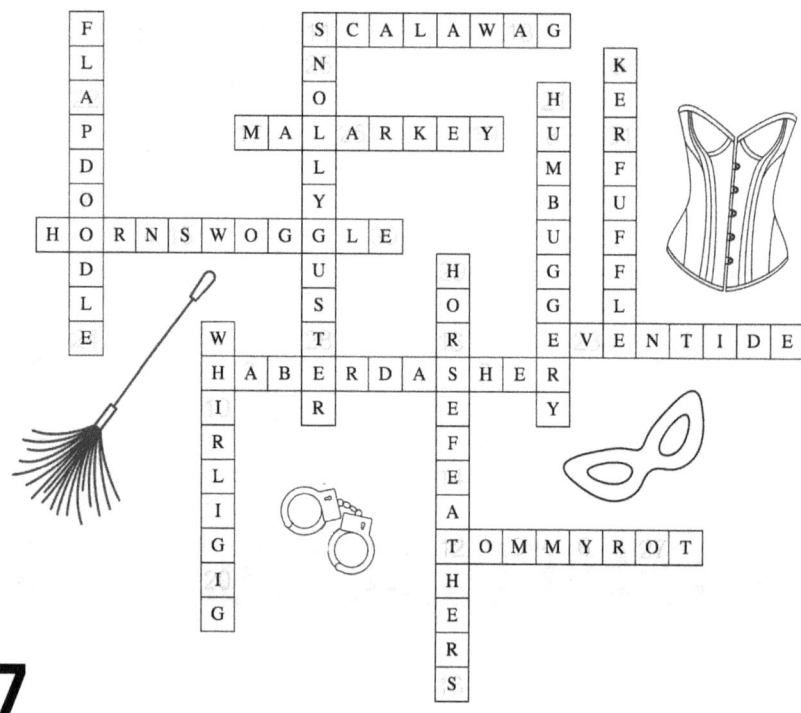

KINKY POP QUIZ

page 46

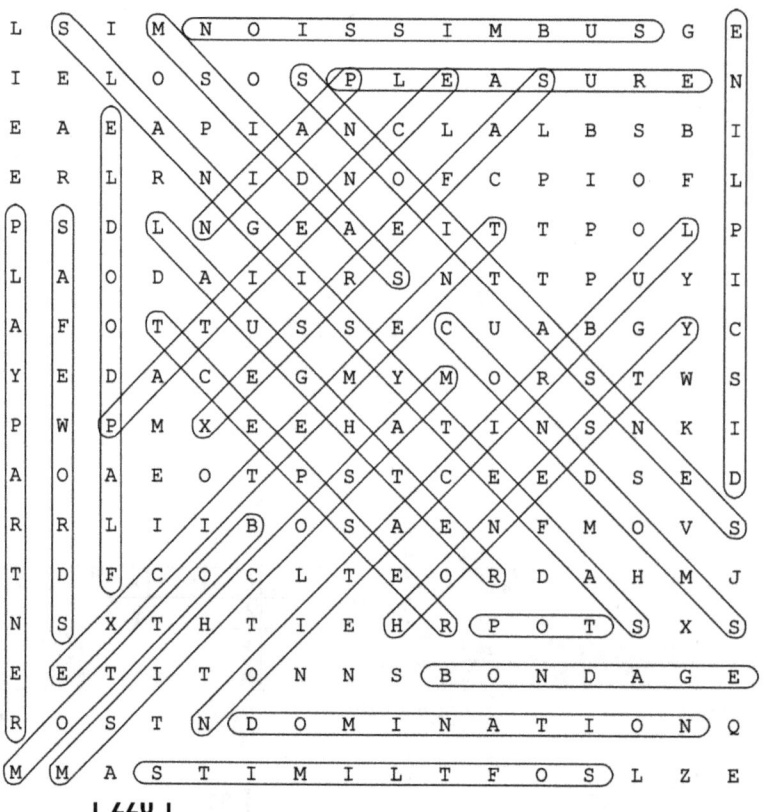

A VERY IMPORTANT MESSAGE

page 50

A	B	C	D	E	F	G	H	I	J	K	L	M	N	O	P	Q	R	S	T	U	V	W	X	Y	Z
6	14	25	16	19	12	18	13	5	26	1	24	20	4	9	11	17	7	3	22	21	23	10	2	8	15

A S   L O N G   A S   I T   I S   S A F E ,

6 3   24 9 4 18   6 3   5 22   5 3   3 6 12 19

S A N E   A N D   C O N S E N S U A L ,   T H E R E

3 6 4 19   6 4 16   25 9 4 3 19 4 3 21 6 24   22 13 19 7 19

I S   N O   R I G H T ;   T H E R E   I S   O N L Y

5 3   4 9   7 5 18 13 22   22 13 19 7 19   5 3   9 4 24 8

W H A T   I S   R I G H T   F O R   Y O U .   A N D

10 13 6 22   5 3   7 5 18 13 22   12 9 7   8 9 21   6 4 16

W H A T   I S   R I G H T   F O R   Y O U   W I L L

10 13 6 22   5 3   7 5 18 13 22   12 9 7   8 9 21   10 5 24 24

C H A N G E   W I T H   T I M E   A N D   A S

25 13 6 4 18 19   10 5 22 13   22 5 20 19   6 4 16   6 3

Y O U   G A I N   K N O W L E D G E   A N D

8 9 21   18 6 5 4   1 4 9 10 24 19 16 18 19   6 4 16

E X P E R I E N C E .

19 2 11 19 7 5 19 4 25 19

FASHION
page 67

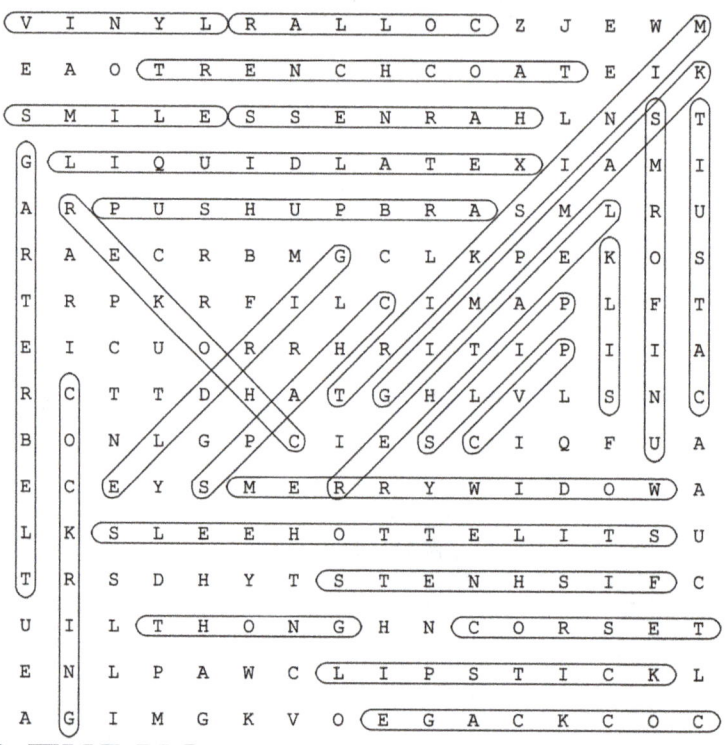

ENJOY THE WRONG TURNS
page 77

KINKY ROLES

page 81

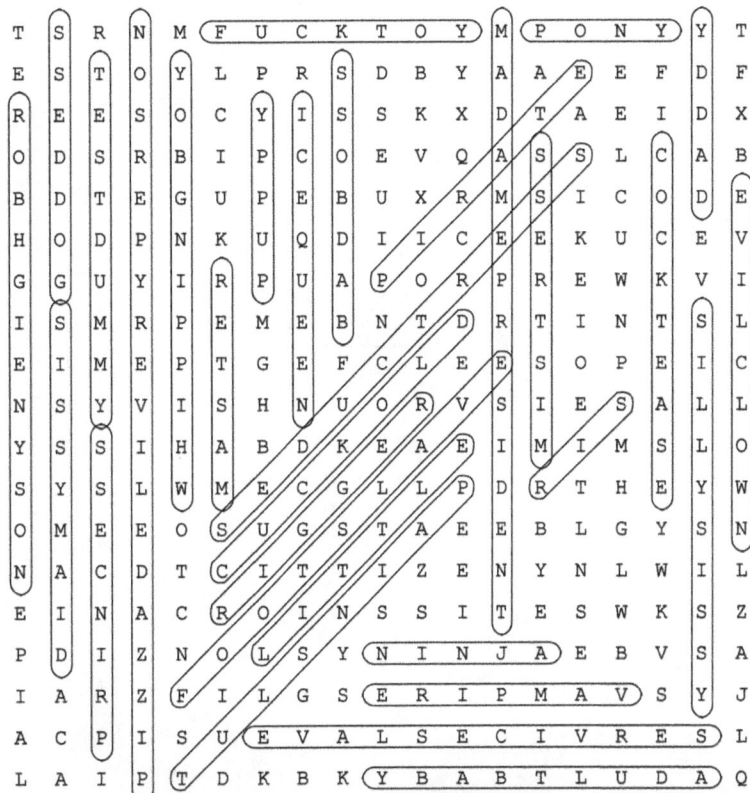

COMMUNICATION IS NEVER A STRAIGHT LINE

page 93

THE CYCLE OF PLAY

page 95

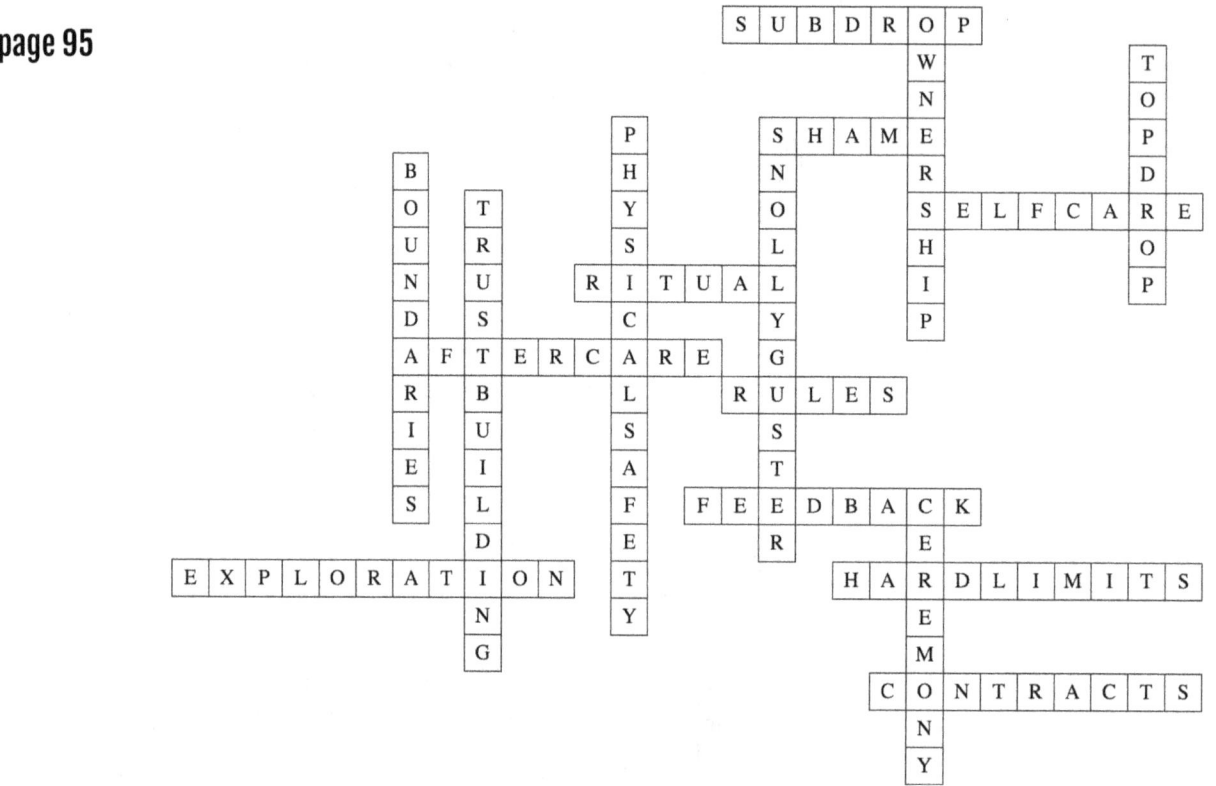

THE EQUIPMENT CLOSET

page 110

Butt plug
Gas Mask
Straight Jacket
Strap on Harness
Leather Restraints
Wooden Paddle
Inflatable Gag
Cat of Nine Tails
Safer Sex Supplies
Bodybag
Handcuffs

Hemp Rope
Nipple Clamps
Posture Collar
Armbinder
Spreader Bar
Human Pony Harness
Bondage Table
Fucking Machine

My safe word is rosebud.

MOVIE NIGHT!

page 156

N **Pretty in Kink** - A teen from the wrong side of the tracks makes her own leather ensemble to impress her wealthy boyfriend
E **The Filth Element** - A futuristic story of a cabbie and a really, really dirty girl.
T **A Fist Full of Collars** - A wandering dungeon monitor plays two rival submissives against each other in a dungeon torn apart by greed, pride, and revenge.
F **Field of Creams** - If you build it, they will cum.
L **Splosh** - A man's short-lived relationship with a mermaid leaves him with a passion for easy to smear foods.
I **Princess Ride** - A princess takes a quick jaunt with a farm boy after he saves her from rodents of unusual size.

A **When Harry Wet Sally** - "I'll have what she's having."
N **Binding Dory** - A woman with memory loss trying to find her way home discovers her real home in ropes.
D **Done in 60 Seconds** - A kinky woman's first date with a vanilla man ends quickly despite his fancy car.

S **Boy Story** - The story of a boy toy and his struggles to accept the Mistress's new boy toy.
P **Piss Congeniality** - An FBI agent must go undercover in a golden shower pageant.
A **Lust in Space** - A navigator has a hard time keeping his ship on track after he notices that the entire crew's space uniforms are basically vinyl catsuits.
N **Indiana Jones and the Lust Crusade** - Archaeologist Jone's eternal search for the woman who will peg him properly.
K **The Mighty Cucks** - A bull must coach a team of cuckolds after getting busted drinking the mistress's bourbon
I **Life of Bi** - While lost at sea, a woman forms an unexpected connection with another woman.
N **A Hard Gay's Night** - Four gay tops from Liverpool spend their first day in the States running from adoring submissives.
G **Gone with the Wand** - A period drama about a high-strung woman discovering the joys of the Hitachi wand.

Answer: Netflix and Spanking

BIG KINKY WORD FIND

page 156

```
E D Y I C O M M U N I C A T I O N L T F
T U A T O G Y Y X L C X E R I A E Y
C N L U W L N A O H E T A O S S
E G P L N B M L P R E N B D T A E
E E E S Y I M I S P E Y I P I N V
G O N Y O N E N G O S H D M R D A
A N T R R U I F R G G C P I A G D L
D T N I R S F E G G J I O N C H S
N N Y A D L C E N S R L K R N B D
O N L H E K N N S A H O V E L S E
B S P D A B W I K T W E S O T T
A T E G U U R B F S R A N I O
A I Y U S K A E A S O Y G A V
Y H A P R K M L T E E R W R E
N C M E P B I C N L T S T T S D
I O L X I B V O O S N S V I E C K E W
R S C H U O N C I Z A Q P E N I W L K
I A W B G F I O I H D E I T G O H R U B
G O M U H T M N Y C R E M R O F G E B R V
```

KINKY VOCABULARY TEST!

page 162

negotiation	unicorn	cuffs	fuck
aftercare	bottom	kinks	pain
pleasure	collar	kneel	play
safeword	fetish	rules	rope
spanking	limits	scene	slut
sub drop	orgasm	shame	whip
top drop	paddle	tease	beg
dungeon	ritual	trust	sex
respect	switch	cage	toy

[226]

IT'S NOT THE END.
IT'S JUST THE BEGINNING...

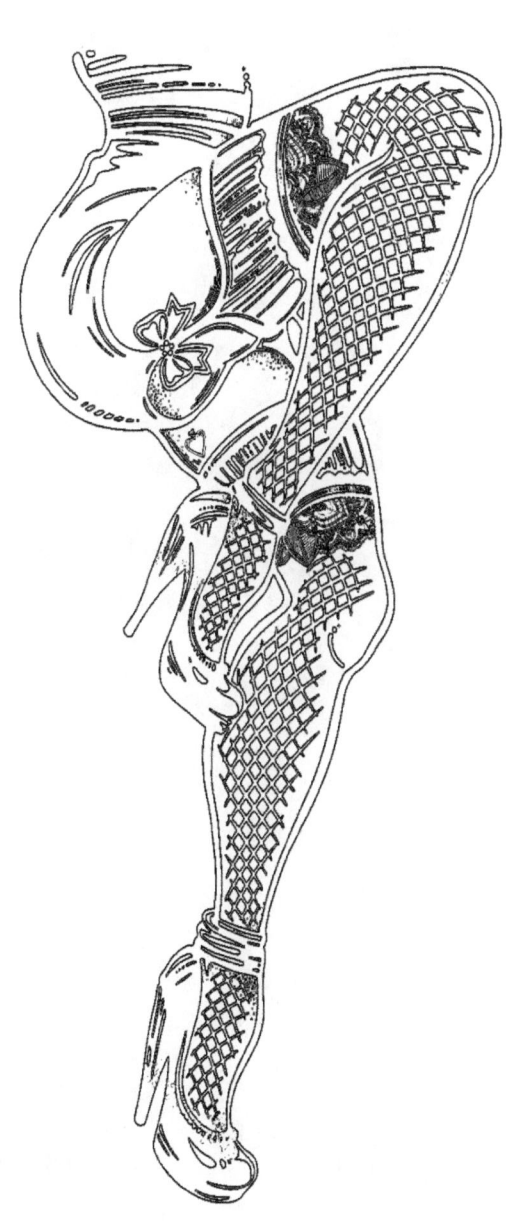

ABOUT PRINCESSA NATASHA STRANGE

Princessa Natasha Strange is a professional dominant, a BDSM educator, a matriarch of many, and an aspiring cult leader with nearly 30 years experience in the world of kink and BDSM.

She is passionate about shame-free, femme-centered BDSM education and women's empowerment, and loves to work with femmes who are curious and ready to take action to change their mindset and start their next chapter. She excels at creating approachable spaces for people to explore scary, intimidating things through the use of puns and laughter.

She delights in all things Disney, small dogs in pajamas, and transforming dude-bros into her sissified playthings.

This book is used as a text book for her online course - Unleash Your Inner Minx: Eight weeks of empowerment, camaraderie, and BDSM education. It's a great place to find others who are interested in learning about kinky fempowerment. To learn more, visit WickedMinx.com.

As the co-owner of Sub Rosa, a fully equipped boutique fetish space located in Portland, Oregon, she and her business partner, Mistress Viola Parker, strive to create an inviting space for others to learn and practice safe, sane, consensual kink and BDSM.

You can read more about her at KittenWithAWhip.com, and about her fetish space, Sub Rosa at SubRosaPDX.com.

Thank you Miss Alice Meow for the illustration on this page. All other art was either purchased from depositphotos.com or traced from her personal collection of photos.